Police Cars

A Photographic History

by Monty McCord

Published by

krause publications

700 East State St.   Iola WI 54990
715-445-2214

Library of Congress Catalog Number: 91-61303
ISBN: 0-87341-171-4
Printed in the United States of America

DEDICATION

To my parents, Barb and Del, who stood by me through good times and bad, and to Kay, my love, whose untiring assistance helped this book become a reality.

ACKNOWLEDGEMENTS

A project of this magnitude would be impossible to complete without the assistance of many people and organizations.

Many individuals generously furnished photographs from their personal collections. Some of these individuals went above and beyond in helping with submissions of photos and information. I owe a special thanks to Charles Chandler, Earl Jensen, Darryl Lindsay and Ned Schwartz.

A number of law enforcement agencies from across the United States also submitted many excellent photos.

I am also greatly indebted to a very special person in my life who spent many hours in helping to prepare the manuscript, Kay Nitz.

My sincere thanks also goes to the following individuals and agencies:

INDIVIDUALS

Judy Ames	Scott Filis	Rick Lenz
John Antonelli	Wayne Fricke	Darryl Lindsay
James E. Ashworth III	Clarence Gibson	Tony Romano
James Baldwin	Walter Gourley	G.E.W. Rupprecht
Al Barnych	Walter Haase	Gil Schugart
Lee Beach	Ric Hallett	Ned Schwartz
Stan & Connie Benjamin	Francis Harr	Domenic Sorbello
Paul Casalese	Jerry Heaseley	Hugh Thomas Jr.
Charles W. Chandler	Jeff Hewlett	Tom Turner
Larry Crutchfield	Lee Hippensteel	George Virgines
W. W. Dalrymple	Hank Jacoby	Paul Weber
Bruce Davisson	Earl W. Jensen	Joe Wicks
Dennis Decker	Terry Jessee	Carl Woehrle
Byran Duncan	Charles Kobel	
Anne Dunn	Mike Kottwitz	
Mike Fay	Bill Krejci	

LAW ENFORCEMENT OFFICIALS

Charles Black—Iowa State Patrol
Susie Boring—Boise, Idaho Police Department
Bill Burkett—Washington State Patrol
Terry Buss—Bakersfield, Calif. Police Department
Vern Campbell—Lincoln, Neb. Police Department
Lt. Ken Elery—Dallas, Texas Police Department
Capt. James Ferrier—Milwaukee, Wis. Police Department
Bob Fitzer—San Francisco, Calif. Police Department
Sgt. Florence Hall—Detroit, Mich. Police Department
Jean Harvey—Tennessee Department of Public Safety
Stephen F. Hatfield—Los Angeles, Calif. Police Department
Maj. John Hershberger—Wichita, Kan. Police Department
Chief Sid Klein—Clearwater, Fla. Police Department
Col. Harold LaGrande—ret.-Nebraska State Patrol
Capt. Donald Lamb—Colorado State Patrol
Clair Lindquist—Lincoln, Neb. Police Department
Lt. A.M. Lundy—Nebraska State Patrol
Tom Lyon—Pennsylvania State Police
Maj. Don Mack—Ohio State Highway Patrol
Phil McArdle—Oakland, Calif. Police Department
Kent R. Milton, California Highway Patrol
Robert Nelson—Minneapolis, Minn. Police Department
Lin Newton—Lawton, Okla. Police Department
Nick Noviello—Nassau County, N.Y. Police Department
Michael Piernicky—Omaha, Neb. Police Department
James Post—(Ret. KCMO PD Sgt.)—Police Car Owners of America
Bob Speed—Baltimore County, Md. Police Department
George Stumpf—United States Marshals Service
David Wells—Texas Department of Public Safety
Joseph Winchell—Albany, N.Y. Police Department

LAW ENFORCEMENT AGENCIES

Alabama Department of Public Safety
Arizona Department of Public Safety
Boys Town, Nebraska Police Department
Denver, Colo. Police Department
Dodge City, Kan. Police Department
Fillmore County, Neb. Sheriff's Department
Florida Highway Patrol
Ford County, Kan. Sheriff's Department
Georgia State Patrol
Hastings, Neb. Police Department
Missouri State Highway Patrol
New Jersey State Police
Ogallala, Neb. Police Department
Saline County, Neb. Sheriff's Department
West Virginia State Police

INDIVIDUALS AND ORGANIZATIONS

Mike Bondarenko, *Police Collectors News*
Charles R. Smith, *Action Era Vehicle*
Chrysler Corp.
Contemporary Historical Vehicle Association Inc.
Ron Grantz, National Automobile History Collection, Detroit Public Library
Roger Haynes, *Tags & Stuff*
Indianapolis Star
Mike Mueller, *Nostalgic Cars*
Joe Vaught and Joe Brady, Diversifleet Inc.

If I have omitted anyone who in any way contributed to this work, I truly apologize. Any omissions of this kind were certainly unintentional.

Anyone interested in the hobby of police vehicles, whether that interest is in the real thing, miniatures, photographs or equipment, should contact:

James Post
Police Car Owners of America
P.O. Box 480021
Kansas City, MO 64148-0021

Police Collectors News
Rural Route One, Box 14
Baldwin, WI 54002

Notice is hereby given that the author will accept photo/information contributions for a possible second edition of *Police Cars*, in care of Krause Publications Inc., 700 East State Street, Iola, WI 54990.

Contents

About the Author

The author is currently a lieutenant with the Hastings, Neb. Police Department. He began his law enforcement career in 1974 as an Adams County deputy sheriff. He served as a Phelps County deputy sheriff before joining the Hastings police in 1978.

Upon entering law enforcement, a hobby of collecting police memorabilia began also.

An avid police historian, McCord published a book in 1982 on his department's history. He has written several articles for *Police Collectors News* on various facets of the hobby. His historical law enforcement articles have appeared in *The Nebraska Police Officer* and *The Texas State Peace Officers Journal*.

He continued building a collection of police insignia for which he has received "best display" awards at collector conventions in Kansas City, Mo., Denver, Colo. and Torrington, Wyo.

A lifelong interest in cars underwent a slight transition, resulting in a certain fondness for police vehicles. He currently owns a 1959 Ford which he outfits with red lights and markings to depict his department's cars of that period. He also owns a 1977 Plymouth which once served with the department.

An avid model police car builder and collector of police vehicle photographs, McCord began working on this book in 1985.

In his spare time, McCord operates a part-time police insignia business in which he designs and sells badges and patches to several different agencies.

He is a member of the Heart of America Police Insignia Collectors Association, The Police Car Owners of America, The Nebraska Crime Prevention Association and the Police Officers Association of Nebraska.

Introduction

The idea for a book of this type came to me several years ago. I have collected photographs of police vehicles for more than 10 years, and as there were no books available on police vehicles through the years, I thought I had a good start on such a project.

My goal in assembling a book like this is to present as many different types of police vehicles as possible. Not only is it interesting to see the variety of vehicle makes used, but also the advancement of equipment and the markings used over the years.

Photos from my own collection as well as those of other police memorabilia collectors are featured in this work. I also sought out the help of many law enforcement agencies around the country who supplied many fine photos. Various other sources were utilized, including libraries and publishing companies.

I have attempted to supply as much accurate information as possible with the photographs presented. Several illustrated reference books were used to aid in the identification of the years and makes of vehicles shown. In addition, I referred to many different law enforcement yearbooks for information. I did find that it was not uncommon for a vehicle to be incorrectly identified in some of these books.

It is my hope that not only will people in the law enforcement profession find this book interesting, but also anyone interested in automotive history. As books on fire trucks, ambulances and military vehicles have been available for several years, this book should fill a long existing void.

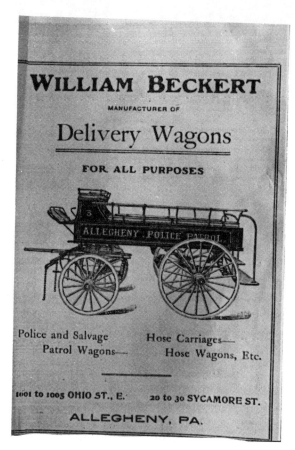

A 1901 advertisement of a police wagon manufacturer.

The earliest "vehicle" used in any type of organized law enforcement work would have to be the trusty horse. Early day lawmen probably considered horses as "primary" transportation. Horses continued their contribution to the police service when they were used to pull the ever present wooden patrol wagons.

These wagons, sometimes referred to as "paddy wagons," were basically a mobile jail cell used to pick up prisoners from policemen who walked a specified beat area.

Even in today's age of computers, horses are still valuable in a number of police functions. Some of these include crowd control, search and rescue, and the patrolling of large parks and mall areas. They are very popular with the public, so community relations could be added to their credits.

The bicycle squad of the Omaha, Neb. Police Department about 1900.

Bicycles were also used in law enforcement work. The first U.S. patent on a pedal driven bicycle was filed in 1866. By 1897, about four million Americans were riding bicycles regularly. We don't see any real use of this vehicle by police until the turn of the century. Bicycles, which could be considered the forerunner of the motorcycle, offered an inexpensive and easy way for a single officer to become more mobile.

In the 1800's, British law enforcers used the "Police Tricycle." The officer, seated between two large wire wheels, would pedal and operate levers to steer a small single front wheel. It's not known how popular these machines were with the "Bobbies."

The first actual motorcycle was invented in 1885 by Gottlieb Daimler, a German engineer. In the United States, the motorcycle got its start in 1901. Bill Harley and Arthur Davidson of Milwaukee, Wis. decided there was a need to take the work out of

The first police motorcycles in Omaha, Neb., circa 1909.

bicycling. By 1903 the joint effort of Harley-Davidson was able to turn out three motorcycles. By 1907, 150 were produced, with an amazing 18,000 being made only 10 years later. By the late 1940s, the Harley-Davidson Co. was so widespread that police in many foreign countries used them including, Australia, South Africa, Korea, Japan and Mexico.

Generally speaking, the first usage of the motorcycle by police was in 1909. During that year, evidence shows that some of the first police departments to use motorcycles were Pittsburgh, Pa., Omaha, Neb. and Houston, Texas, to name a few. Ever since then, the motorcycle has been a common tool of the law enforcement trade.

Motorcycles have been used by police in various ways since they were invented, but they've had considerable success in traffic enforcement work. Their ability to get through congested areas is unsurpassed. Although other U.S. manfacturers, most notably Henderson and Indian, produced popular police motorcycles, only Harley-Davidson has survived. In modern times we see numerous foreign cycles (mostly Japanese) being used by American lawmen. Name brands such as Kawasaki, Yamaha, Moto Guzzi, BMW, Honda and Suzuki are common. Some of these, however, are being manufactured in the United States.

The origin of the police car is really a contradiction in terms as it was the truck that was the first motorized four-wheel vehicle utilized by law enforcement. These early police vehicles closely resembled the horse-drawn wagons but without horses.

The thinking of the time on "horseless" vehicles is illustrated by a statement made in 1909 by the police chief of Louisville, Ky., who said, "The Louisville Police Department is so progressive that we no longer have the need for the horse, and now have three power-driven vehicles in service." The argument against the horse-drawn patrol wagons rested in three main areas: officer safety, efficiency and cost.

When a beat officer arrested an unruly person, he not only had to drag him several blocks in order to locate a telephone or call box, he sometimes had to wait for up to an hour before the patrol wagon could arrive. An uncooperative prisoner would be difficult enough to tolerate, but an unruly crowd would sometimes gather, taunting the unfortunate policeman. By the same reasoning, if an emergency call came into the station requiring a number of officers, response to the call was delayed until the patrol wagon returned. When answering a call of a crime in progress, the culprits would often be long gone by the time the wagonload of policemen arrived. By 1910, a police official predicted, "The day is coming soon that no police department will be considered up-to-date without the automobile."

The average patrol wagon with horses and related equipment cost almost $2,000. The cost of a power-driven vehicle was only slightly higher, but when the department sold it, they could recover a respectable amount of their initial investment. A worn-out horse-drawn wagon was almost worthless. Estimates made at the time stated that the average cost to operate a horse-

This early 1900s paddy wagon has mesh screens on the insides of the windows to discourage early departures.

drawn wagon was $50 per month. In comparison, it was said the monthly cost of an automobile was $20.

Not all policemen served as a driver of the horse-drawn or power-driven vehicles. Certain dependable officers were chosen to undertake rudimentary training, not only in operating, but maintaining these machines. Even though still a "policeman," their titles would be "chauffeur" or "driver." In some cases, as in Omaha, Neb. the officers' badges were inscribed, "Patrol Driver." They usually received the same pay as the other policemen.

Along with the gasoline engine, electrical power supplied by crude batteries was used to power these early machines. We know electric patrol wagons were used by the Los Angeles, Calif. police in 1904 and the Oakland police in 1907. These were found to be too expensive when comparing batteries and recharging costs to that of gasoline at the time.

Some of the companies that produced these early patrol trucks were Cadillac, Oldsmobile, Stoddard-Dayton, White, GMC, Pope-Hartford and Locomobile.

The duties of the patrol trucks was extended out of necessity to include transportation of the sick and injured. It was common in the early 1900s for the police to furnish ambulance service within their jurisdictions. An example would be the Waterbury, Conn. police, who had a specially built Pope-Hartford for this purpose. The vehicle was used for both patrol and ambu-

This early 1900s touring car was used by the Omaha, Neb. police.

lance duties. Baltimore, Md. police reported for the year 1909, that out of 21,000 calls for service, over 2,200 were ambulance calls.

Autos used for patrol were also coming into use, but they still weren't as popular as the trucks that could accommodate several officers or prisoners. The autos usually used were of a touring type because they had substantial seating capacity.

These were especially effective, it was said, for detectives in plainclothes to use cars with no special markings. They would then be able to approach criminals without being detected.

In the 1920s, law enforcement officials discovered the need for faster, more rugged cars in which to battle gangsters during Prohibition. Automakers such as Gardner, Lincoln, Cadillac, Buick, Hudson and Studebaker all offered special police vehicles. One of the most famous "police specials," called the Arizona Sheriff, was made by Studebaker.

It was not uncommon for police cars of this era to be outfitted with bullet-proof glass and metal plating and be armed with machine guns. One such car, nicknamed "Leaping Lena," was used by the Denver, Colo. police. This Cadillac touring car featured armor plating, front- and rear-mounted machine guns and extra lights. Long, wide runningboards allowed several officers to ride. The car was capable of ramming without being badly damaged, thanks to the front bumper which was made from a piece of railroad track!

Dollars were tight in the 1930s, and as a result the large expensive police specials that met with acceptance in the '20s lost some popularity. Law enforcement agencies all over the country looked for less expensive but reliable patrol cars. Henry Ford seemed to have the answer in 1932 when he introduced the new 65 hp flathead V-8 engine. The Ford coupes purchased by the California Highway Patrol cost about $490 each. They could sustain 75 mph, which was fast enough to catch most of the cars on the road.

Ford's "police special" for 1932 was centered on the Standard phaeton model, a four-door convertible, which allowed an easy range of fire for machine gun-wielding officers.

The availability of automobiles was reduced during World War II, as the manufacturers geared up to produce military hardware. New models weren't available from 1943 through 1945. In 1946 the supply could not begin to meet the demand for new cars, so law enforcement agencies were forced to use whatever makes they could find. The V-8 Ford was still very popular, especially because of its lower price.

Although Oldsmobile and Cadillac were outfitted with the overhead valve V-8 engine in 1949, Ford continued production of its flathead V-8 until 1954. At this time

State-of-the-art police interceptor—1932. Ford had the ultimate chase car in 1932 with the introduction of the flathead V-8 engine. This one worked for the California Highway Patrol.

A trooper of the Pennsylvania State Police uses the two-way radio in his 1954 Ford patrol car. The microphone is the old telephone handset type.

Ford bravely met the competition for the police car market when they offered the 256 cubic inch "Thunderbird" engine. This special police option was rated at 160 hp.

Ford cornered the police market, if only for a short time. Chevrolet, Pontiac and Plymouth were offered with new V-8 engines in 1955. Manufacturers seemed to be in a race for largest engine size and horsepower rating.

Through the 1950s and 1960s, names like "Patroller," "Pursuit Special," and "Interceptor" became well known as police cars. The large four-door patrol cars with massive engines were prevalent well into the 1970s. Some common engine sizes were the 440, 400, 383 and 429 cubic inch models. In 1972 the Los Angeles police puchased over 500 AMC Matadors, which were equipped with 401 cubic inch engines. We should remember this cruiser from the last seasons of TV's "Adam-12." The behemoths of this era were to go down in history as being some of the fastest regular-production police service vehicles.

Around 1974 the Los Angeles County Sheriff's Department tested the Chevrolet Nova, eventually placing a fleet of them on patrol duty. By 1977, Chevrolet billed the Nova as the best selling compact police car in the country. The largest user of the Nova was the Jacksonville, Fla. Sheriff's Department, who purchased 227 units.

Chevrolet replaced the Nova in 1979 with the Malibu as their compact police offering.

Chrysler Corp. entered this market with the release of the Plymouth Volare in 1977. Combining its smaller size with a 360 cubic inch 195 hp engine, it was a fast pursuit car.

The 1979 Camaro Z-28 was tested by the California Highway Patrol with somewhat disappointing results. Its use was not continued primarily because of engine troubles.

A non-traditional car "pinned on a badge" in 1979 when the California Highway Patrol put 12 Chevrolet Camaro Z-28s into service. These were stock Z-28s except they were fitted with more restrictive emission control devices, which reduced the 350 cubic inch engine's horsepower. Problems plagued this sporty cruiser, however, as all 12 had to have their engines replaced. Shotguns, normally carried in a vertical mount attached to the dash, had to have their stocks shortened to fit. The car's interior had a very limited amount of space for equipment or prisoners. The long doors made them dangerous to open when making vehicle stops on busy highways. These problems, as well as others, assured that the use of the Z-28s wouldn't be continued after the intial group reached the end of their service.

After several years of searching for a car that could catch fast foreign sports cars, the California Highway Patrol found what they wanted in the 302 cubic inch Ford Mustang. The agency put the Mustang through a series of severe tests, including running the car at top speed for several miles without trouble and hard braking from those high speeds. After successfully passing these and other tests, the California Highway Patrol bought 400 specially equipped

1982 Mustangs for patrol use. Advertising for the car read, "This Ford chases Porshes for a living." The only drawback of the Mustang has been the lack of room for prisoners, but the California Highway Patrol has plenty of four-door sedans to supplement them. The California Highway Patrol liked the Mustang so much that they now have over 600 in service. As in the past, this agency started a trend that spread across the United States, as more than 25 states now use the Mustang.

The car that satisfied the California Highway Patrol's need for a fast pursuit car was the Ford Mustang.

The 1987 GMC Safari van was tested by the San Francisco, Calif. police.

1987 marked the year that the mini-van was tested for patrol use. The San Francisco Police put a GMC Safari van on the street for 30 days. The van, equipped with a 4.3 liter V-6 engine, performed very well and passed the tests it was given. Although test results showed the mini-van performed acceptably for patrol, it isn't commonly used for this purpose. It has, however, found a place in law enforcement in many special areas such as: prisoner transport, mobile crime labs, Special Weapons and Tactics Teams, K-9 teams, underwater recovery teams and community relations, to name just a few. It seems the possible uses for mini-vans is nearly unlimited. Interestingly, foreign police forces have utilized vans for a number of years.

The search for a new type of police vehicle continues. The Ford Motor Co. engages law enforcement agencies such as the Dearborn, Mich. Police Department and the Arizona Highway Patrol as test beds for their vehicles. The Dearborn department and the Wayne County, Mich. Sheriff's Department tested Lincoln Continental Town Cars on patrol. Talk about a plush office for the patrolman! Surprisingly, officers seemed to prefer regular sedans such as the Crown Victoria.

In 1988, Ford sent five special Thunderbirds to Arizona for the highway patrol to test. The fully marked units were equipped with 3.8 liter supercharged engines, which reportly made pursuits shorter than normal! A restyled 1989 Thunderbird, being tested by the Dearborn Police, is equipped with the same type of engine.

One of five 1988 Ford Thunderbirds being tested by the Arizona Highway Patrol. These experimental cruisers are powered by a supercharged 3.8 liter engine.

The Dodge Diplomat was dropped after the 1989 model year, leaving Chrysler Corp. out of the police market. The Diplomat was used in large numbers throughout the 1980s.

In 1989, the Wayne County, Mich. Sheriff's Department was called on again by Ford to test a new police package Taurus that they offered for the first time in 1990. The Taurus is available with a 3.8 liter V-6 engine with sequential electronic fuel injection. Early indications would suggest that the mid-size Taurus has found its niche in the field of law enforcement.

1991 brings the continued and well established success of the Ford Mustang as a patrol car. The new Chevrolet Caprice has been completely restyled with a more aerodynamic body.

Chevrolet also challenges the Mustang with the release of the Camaro RS "special pursuit package." As of this writing, the Nebraska State Patrol, for one, has placed an order for a small group of these new cruisers. Only time will tell if they will make a better showing than they did in California in 1979.

Police officials have varying opinions as to the use of "non-traditional" cars. Some feel that nothing other than the standard four-door sedan specially equipped for police use should be utilized. There seems to be an underlying concern about how officers will operate a non-traditional cruiser. The obvious increased use of these vehicles seems to negate such thinking. Effective traffic enforcement is already a major trophy of the Mustangs in more than half of our nation's highway patrol agencies. There is, and will be, a continuing need for sedans that can accommodate prisoners for transporting.

What the future will bring is unknown. Perhaps we will return to the days when the beat officer had to call for the horse-drawn paddy wagon to pick up his prisoner. The beat officer may be calling from the comfort of his small high powered pursuit car, and the paddy wagon may be a mini-van that more closely resembles a spacecraft. In any event, it will be fascinating to see, with all of the different types of vehicles being tested, what will become the police car of the future.

One of the 1990 Ford Taurus police package cars in service with the Lincoln, Neb. police.

Chevrolet introduced its sleek Camaro RS in a police package in 1991 to compete with Ford's Mustang. This Z-28 has been in service with the Saline County, Neb. Sheriff's Department for the past couple of years. One of the new police Camaros was recently added to the department.

1

The Early Years

The Oakland, Calif. police obtained their first patrol wagon around 1880. It sported rarely seen fenders over the rear wheels.

An 1880s San Francisco police wagon is shown to local dignitaries.

An 1880s patrol wagon of the Lincoln, Neb. Police Department. Looks like the whole department must be in this photo.

Three Los Angeles police officers pose in their patrol wagon. This photo from the 1880s features very ornate "Police Patrol" markings.

These Dallas, Texas police officers pose for a photo, about 1890.

Looks like these Kansas City, Mo. policemen had their hands full with this load of lawbreakers. Photo taken in 1890.

This light patrol wagon, complete with brass railings, is manned by Washington D.C. police, about 1890.

Police patrol wagon #1 was photographed at 11th and Dodge Streets, Omaha, Neb. about 1900.

This Dallas, Texas police paddy wagon features "state of the art" emergency horn and heavy metal screen sides.

A 1900s Detroit police touring car parked outside an Oldsmobile dealership.

A Kansas City, Mo. police motorcycle squad pose outside station Number 6.

An early 1900s motorized paddy wagon fitted with the emergency equipment of the day. The unusual window coverings appear to be venetian blinds.

The driver of this 1905 GMC truck obviously has a good range of view. This truck was used for hauling large amounts of property and/or evidence.

New York City Police Department used this motorized paddy wagon in 1905.

A large patrol truck of the Chicago Police Department. Circa 1905.

About 1908 the Oakland, Calif. police got their first motorcycle. This early Indian more closely resembles a bicycle!

This Dallas, Texas "Police Squad" truck was used about 1910. This unique vehicle has a large spotlight and was handy for transporting groups of officers to trouble spots.

These two Oakland, Calif. police officers appear to be ready for patrol in their 1914 Model T Ford.

Pictured is the first motorcycle squad of the Oakland, Calif. Police Department, taken in 1914. If was found that patrol cars were not as efficient for traffic control in congested areas as cycles, therefore this squad was formed.

A 1914 touring car with right-hand drive is being operated by a captain of the Los Angeles Police Department.

This 1915 motorcycle patrolman pulls over a driver. "Was I speeding?"

This 1915 GMC truck was used by dog catchers on the Detroit, Mich. Police Department. The box was built with many separate compartments to accommodate stray animals.

This variety of vehicles, mostly Model Ts, was used by the Dallas, Texas police about 1915.

The 1917 Detroit Police Department "open" patrol wagon back on regular duties.

A 1917 Detroit, Mich. Police Department "open" patrol wagon fitted for a parade.

These Detroit, Mich. police officers pose proudly with an early patrol wagon which has been outfitted for winter with tire chains.

This Detroit, Mich. patrol wagon is marked simply, "No. 5." This wagon could seat a large number of officers and/or prisoners. The canvas side curtains could be lowered during inclement weather.

The Omaha, Neb. Police Department used this slightly more modern enclosed type patrol wagon in 1909.

This photo is a wagon owned by the Omaha, Neb. Police Department. These officers left the top off to enjoy the weather.

Patrol wagon #8 of the San Francisco, Calif. police, about 1910.

A patrol wagon of the Baltimore, Md. police in 1880. The large brass bell beside the driver served as one of the first warning devices for emergency equipment.

This photo of an 1880s patrol wagon of the Kansas City, Mo. police shows something unusual: Their horses are wearing badges, too!

This photo, taken about 1885, shows New York City police officers posing outside the 61st Precinct headquarters.

This 1890 photo of the Hartford, Conn. police shows them ready for action in their open type police wagon featuring a "baby" Gatling gun. The gun was for "riot use."

To know which car to buy, the Oakland, Calif. Police Department held a road race consisting of Pope-Hartfords, Cadillacs, Appersons and many others. The Pope-Hartfords came in first and second so two were purchased by the department. One was converted into a combination patrol/wagon/ambulance, while the other (pictured) was used as an emergency car for VIPs.

This two-seater Autocar of the Oakland, Calif. Police Department featured Fisk tires and a four-cylinder engine. 1906.

This 1908 While Steamer of the Omaha, Neb. Police Department was destroyed by fire in October 1908. The garage fire also claimed the horse patrol wagons, an emergency rig and six horses.

At the turn of the century, the Omaha, Neb. police operated this ambulance wagon and emergency rig. The emergency rig was used for calls which required immediate response.

The Oakland, Calif. Police Department found that batteries and re-charges for this 1907 electric patrol wagon cost $1,000 per year, which was higher than the cost of fuel for gas-driven vehicles.

The first electric patrol wagon of the Los Angeles, Calif. Police Department. This vehicle, purchased in 1904, cost $2,500 and was used as an ambulance and patrol wagon.

This is the rear view of a Los Angeles Calif. electric patrol wagon taken in 1904. This vehicle, as you can see, also served as an ambulance.

2

1920s

This 1920s paddy wagon may have been used by the Chicago, Ill. Police Department.

Well armed Dallas, Texas policemen pose with a 1920s era touring car.

A Los Angeles, Calif. police sergeant poses with his powerful patrol unit in the 1920s.

A late 1920s paddy wagon.

Fully loaded Model T touring cars of the New York State Police in the early 1920s. The sign attached to the radiator of the center car is the only police marking.

Patrol cars of the Los Angeles, Calif. police in the 1920s.

Taking a police radio call isn't what it used to be!

This Model T coupe was the first motorized police car for the Albany, N.Y. Police Department.

Nassau County, N.Y. police seize an illegal still during prohibition. Police trucks like this one were used extensively for transporting confiscated goods to the station.

Detroit, Mich. police officials ride in a patrol car around 1920.

A 1920 touring car of the Albany, N.Y. Police Department.

An apparent difference of opinion is continuing as this 1920 Detroit, Mich. police tow truck prepared to do its job.

These Detroit, Mich. policemen seem to be ready for patrol on a cold winter day. This photo was taken about 1920.

This well-known photo shows Detroit, Mich. Police Commissioner Walter Stick with a 1921 Ford Model T police car. This car is generally known as the world's first radio police car. Note the primitive antenna on the roof.

Minneapolis, Minn. police officers pose by their cars on a cold winter day in 1924 at Bryant Station.

This 1925 Ford Model T roadster was a detective bureau car with the Nassau County, N.Y. Police Department. Note the "P.D." marking on the door.

This Ford Model T was one of the first patrol cars used by the Nassau County, N.Y. police when the department was originated in 1925. The police commissioner ordered that the tops were to be down in all but the most severe weather. Because of this and the fact that the cars had no heaters, officers had to wear very heavy coats.

Illinois State Police and their new Chrysler 70 coupes in 1927.

Patrol car #23, a 1928 Chevrolet convertible, of the Nassau County, N.Y. police.

An inspector of the California Highway Patrol poses with his unit, a 1927 Gardner.

A 1929 Dodge Brothers patrol wagon of the Hamtramck, Mich. Police Department. That year, commercial chassis represented about 20 percent of Dodge's output, a business which grew out of the firm's production of troop carriers, combat machines, screen-sided panel trucks, and ambulances during World War I. The wagon shown here had a 140-inch wheelbase. The 208 cubic inch engine was rated at 63 horsepower.

In the past, police departments commonly operated ambulances along with their duties. This 1929 Reo was used by the force in San Diego, Calif.

New York City policeman John McCann served from 1926 to 1944. He is shown here, a member of Motorcycle Precinct #1, in the late 1920s.

Motorcycle highway patrol units from Pennsylvania in the 1920s.

Pennsylvania State Police (Highway Patrol) motorcycles with sidecars in the 1920s.

Los Angeles, Calif. police motorcycle officers pose with their mounts in the 1920s.

A photo taken in 1920 shows motorcycles of the Minneapolis, Minn. Police Department.

A California Highway Patrol officer poses on his 1920 flathead Indian Chief.

An Omaha, Neb. police "pill box" crew, circa 1925. In 1923 Omaha started experimenting with "state of the art" methods of police work. The "pill boxes" were one of them. These were small garages located at different spots and manned by two officers. The garage housed a police motorcycle with sidecar, a desk, a restroom, and a telephone with a direct line to police headquarters. The city had nine of these spread around the city and claimed any call could be reached in five minutes or less. These officers were credited with many arrests, including burglars, hold-up men, and safe blowers.

In 1923 the "State Highway Patrol" was formed in Pennsylvania. Shown here is one of the first motorcycles they used.

Sergeant Beckett and Patrolman Hanlon of the Nassau County, N.Y. police. These guys are ready for duty with their 1925 Harley-Davidson motorcycle.

These motorcycle units of the Oakland, Calif. Police Department promote traffic safety in a 1926 parade.

*1929 Ford roadsters of the Hastings, Neb. Police Department shown with the depart-
ment at the city auditorium. The doors read, "Police Patrol No. 1 and 2 Hastings,
Nebr." The cars were green with black fenders.*

A 1920 Denver, Colo. police paddy wagon.

Emergency crews and cars of the Omaha, Neb. Police Department in 1925.

"The Time to Prevent Accidents is Now," proclaims the message on this 1929 Chevrolet sedan delivery. The truck was used by the Wichita, Kan. police for safety education.

This heavily equipped roadster served in the Dallas, Texas Police Fire Signal Department.

A 1920 San Francisco, Calif. paddy wagon.

The hood of this Ford Model T seems to be just right for transporting the saddle of these "modern" Texas Rangers.

An Omaha, Neb. police armored car parked in front of the Orpheum theatre in 1925. "Money Car" service began in 1925 by the Omaha Police Department because of many payroll holdups in the Omaha area. Police would provide armed escort to any merchant free of charge. This service was discontinued in 1932 due to budget constraints.

This is paddy wagon No. 3 belonging to the Albany, N.Y. Police Department. It was used in the 1920s.

The Sandusky, Ohio police used this Overland truck around 1925.

Wichita, Kan. policemen pose beside their Ford Model A touring car. Note the light on the front of the radiator and the stop light on the side of the cowling.

The fleet of solo motorcycle patrols of the Omaha, Neb. Police Department. This photo was taken in 1925.

A couple of Kansas City, Mo. Police Department motorcycles in the 1920s.

This paddy wagon was used by the Kansas City, Mo. Police Department in the 1920s.

A Ford Model T touring car of the Kansas City, Mo. Police Department.

A California Highway Patrolman leans on his 1929 Hudson coupe, one of the original C.H.P. patrol cars. The C.H.P. was formed in 1929.

3

Officers stop for a photo at an early Arizona Highway Patrol station.

A large truck was used by the Nassau County, N.Y. Police Department for displaying this traffic safety billboard.

A future patrolman stands on the runningboard of this Idaho state policeman's Ford Model A coupe.

Detroit, Mich. policemen shown here in front of the municipal garage with their Ford Model As.

This West Virginia police motorcycle officer monitors traffic in the late 1930s.

Motorcycles as far as the eye can see. Los Angeles Police Department's traffic division in the 1930s.

This Missouri state trooper employs a retaining strap on his cap when operating his motorcycle. Notice his equipment includes a first aid kit.

Officers of the Pennsylvania State Police in the 1930s pose with their Indian motorcycles.

An Indian motorcycle and patrolman of the Ohio Highway Patrol—1930s.

This heavy truck, a 1930 International, was used by the Nassau County, N.Y. police.

Unit Number 8 of the Michigan State Police, a 1930 Packard touring car.

San Francisco, Calif. motorcycle officers lined up in front of the city hall for a photo about 1930. It's quite an impressive assembly.

Circa 1930 Ford Model As of the Minneapolis, Minn. Police Department at the old gateway station.

A smartly uniformed Dallas, Texas police officer proudly sits on number 6. Photo circa 1930.

This California Highway Patrolman poses at home for a photo with his 1930 Indian motorcycle.

1930 motorcycle officer of the Oakland, Calif. Police Department.

At first glance this 1931 Mack appears to be a fire truck! No so; it's a unit of the New York City Police Emergency Services Unit in the 1930s.

California Highway Patrol officers pose with their 1931 Dodge coupes.

Lincoln, Neb. police, tired of outdated chase cars, purchased these two Ford Model As in 1931. Extra metal panels were ordered with these to make them more bullet resistant.

In 1933, the California Highway Patrol used this Graham coupe.

This 1934 Ford coupe is marked on the doors, "State of Idaho Law Enforcement Department." (Idaho State Police.)

A 1934 Chevrolet coupe of the Nassau County, N.Y. Police Department. The door emblem reads: "Police Radio-32-N.C.P.D."

Traffic safety has been a concern for some time as evidenced by this 1934 Chevrolet sedan delivery. The West Virginia State Police used this vehicle in promoting traffic safety.

A group of Lincoln, Neb. motorcycle policemen. Photo taken about 1934.

*A California Highway Patrolman astride his Harley-Davidson on a chilly day in 1934.
Do you suppose that scarf is part of his uniform?*

A sharp 1934 Chevrolet roadster of the West Virginia State Police.

Your driving would improve if you saw this 1935 Ford in your rearview mirror. This car was used by the Washington State Patrol.

80

A lineup of Wichita, Kan. policemen and their patrol cars, mostly 1934 Plymouths.

A long line of brand new 1935 Chevrolets ready for service with the Missouri State Highway Patrol.

Members of the Detroit, Mich. Police Department pose proudly with their new fleet of 1935 Hudson Terraplanes.

This 1935 Ford coupe of the Nassau County, N.Y. Police Department was assigned to highway patrol duties. These units were known as the "Ghost Patrol."

Officers of the Los Angeles, Calif. police demonstrate the handy flip-out windshield on their 1935 Plymouth cruiser.

Albany, N.Y. police used this 1935 Terraplane coupe.

The equipment carried in this 1935 Chevrolet of the Ohio Highway Patrol includes kerosene lanterns, a first aid kit, a blanket, an axe, and a fire extinguisher.

This dutiful policeman is no doubt taking his time in giving these distressed citizens proper directions. Police work could be enjoyable, even in 1936!

This 1936 Chevrolet sedan delivery served in the identification bureau of the Nassau County, N.Y. Police Department.

The Washington State Patrol used sedan deliveries extensively, including this 1936 Ford. They served well as a patrol vehicle, ambulance, and temporary jail.

A 1936 Ford phaeton of the New Jersey State Police.

This immaculate 1936 Ford served with the Milwaukee, Wis. police.

A 1936 GMC paddy wagon of the Milwaukee, Wis. Police Department.

A front view of a West Virginia State Police 1936 Ford roadster showing the markings and lights.

A 1937 Chevrolet of the San Francisco, Calif. Police Department. The SFPD style door emblem is still used today in San Francisco.

A 1936 Ford sedan pulling a "port of entry" trailer at the state capital. These ports of entry were for the collection of taxes from truck traffic as well as for public relations for tourists.

This New York City Police paddy wagon was used from 1937 to 1940. The Reo Speed Wagon was dark green with black fenders.

A 1937 Pontiac and 1936 Ford of the California Highway Patrol. Note the early "E" license plates.

A 1937 DeSoto police car. Note early radio microphone.

A row of 1937 Chevrolet four-door sedans parked in front of the fifth precinct in Minneapolis, Minn.

This 1937 Plymouth coupe served with the Nassau County, N.Y. Police Department.

The Detroit, Mich. Police Department used this fine 1937 Lincoln Zephyr, which featured a gun barrel port in the right side of the windshield.

This factory photo shows a 1938 Plymouth coupe being inspected by Detroit police officials. Notice the New York City Police Department markings.

A 1938 Buick and a 1937 Chrysler Imperial of the California Highway Patrol.

1938 and 1937 Buicks of the Texas Department of Public Safety. Texas Ranger Col. Homer Garrison is in the dark suit.

A piece of sheet metal riveted to the door of this 1938 Ford provided markings for the Texas Rangers. Modern Texas Ranger vehicles are not marked.

A 1938 Chevrolet sedan utilized by the Nebraska Safety Patrol. When pulling over a motorist, the patrolman would pull alongside the violator and turn on the fender stop light.

This 1938 Ford one-ton panel truck served as a paddy wagon for the San Francisco, Calif. police. It has a 134-inch wheelbase with optional dual rear wheels.

Here's another example of a safety education unit. This 1938 Plymouth belonging to the Detroit, Mich. Police Department features an unusual roof-mounted sound speaker.

This 1938 Chevrolet truck was a communications unit for emergency situations.

A 1938 Chrysler of the famous Texas Rangers. Although cars have made transportation easier, the trusty horse is still used today by the Rangers when necessary.

A 1938 Ford of the Colorado Courtesy Patrol (State Patrol). When the Colorado patrol was organized, it was decided to paint the patrol cars and motorcycles orange and black. The idea was so disliked, it was only a matter of days before this silver and black paint scheme was adopted.

"First fleet of Chevrolets, Georgia State Patrol, Feb. 17, 1938."

A 1938 Ford of the Texas Highway Patrol.

1938 Plymouths like this one were replacing motorcycles in the Pennsylvania Motor Police at the time this photo was taken. These patrol cars look white, but were actually light gray.

Two Ohio highway patrolmen display the equipment they carry in their 1938 Ford patrol car.

A 1939 Chevrolet of the Pennsylvania Motor Police.

These 1939 Ford coupes are part of the Washington State Patrol Safety Education Unit, Division of Accident Prevention.

By 1939 the Idaho State Police were using bold markings, including the state shape, as on this Chevrolet.

Motorcycles and patrol cars of the San Mateo, Calif. Police Department shown outside the station house in 1939.

This 1939 Ford "black and white" served with the Los Angeles, Calif. Police Department.

This 1939 Dodge served in the safety division of the Detroit, Mich. Police Department. It looks like that officer's spent some time telling people how to drive safely in snow and ice.

1937 Ford of the Colorado Courtesy Patrol. Note the mud and snow tires on the front to help with traction.

As this 1938 Plymouth brochure proclaims, "The car that stands up the best," which included police work.

Chief Kelley of Kansas went on to explain that they put 85,000 miles on their 1934 Plymouth before an overhaul was necessary. "50,000 miles were put on the car before the pan was ever off. That's a record for any car in police service!"

Patrolmen posing with units at state patrol headquarters in Denver, Colo. in 1935.

This well-marked 1934 Ford sedan served as a safety car for the Arizona Highway Patrol.

The Lincoln, Neb. Police Department first used one-way radios in 1933 Ford sedans like this one.

This 1936 Ford truck carried special lighting equipment to the scene for the Nassau County, N.Y. Police Department.

Part of the "Original 44" members of the Nebraska Safety Patrol pose with their first patrol cars, 1937 Fords.

This International truck was used by the Pennsylvania State Police Communications Division in the 1930s.

This 1934 Chrysler Airflow made a unique patrol car for the California Highway Patrol.

New York state policemen relax against their 1937 Ford phaeton.

A Kansas City, Mo. police motorcycle officer beside a 1934 Plymouth. Both vehicles are assigned to the traffic division.

The Sheffield, Ala. police pose here with a suspected bootlegger and his 1933 Chevrolet sedan.

These California Highway Patrolmen pose with a fellow officer and his 1937 DeSoto. The patrolman on the left appears to be "off duty" judging from his uniform.

4

1940s

This Milwaukee, Wis. policeman apparently patrolled on his Harley-Davidson in the winter as well as in the summer months. The canvas fairing provided some protection for him.

This armored vehicle, used in the 1940s by the Milwaukee, Wis. police, was so heavy it easily wore out its tires.

Female traffic officers of the San Francisco, Calif. police pose with their motorcycles at unit headquarters, 110 Clara Street, in the 1940s.

These 1940 Ford Standard Fordors were Kansas City, Mo. police accident investigation units. They sold new for about $750 each.

This Ford truck served the Texas Department of Public Safety as a field communications unit in the 1940s.

This armored truck was used by the Minneapolis, Minn. police in the 1940s.

This Harley-Davidson of the Missouri State Highway Patrol performed its duties in the 1940s.

A Harley-Davidson motorcycle of the California Highway Patrol in the late 1930s-early 1940s.

These ex-military Jeeps were used for regular patrol duty after World War II by the Lincoln, Neb. police. They were repainted black with white trim, but the top and interior remained olive drab green.

This sharp-looking 1940 Ford Standard Tudor was in service with the Wichita, Kan. Police Department. The type of stoplight shown at the front of the door began being used in the mid-1930s.

This Stewart was the first bomb unit of the Milwaukee, Wis. police. This picture is from 1940.

A pilot project was initiated by the Nebraska Safety Patrol in 1940 to increase visibility. The top of this 1940 Chevrolet was painted white and named "Guinea Pig." Public reaction was so favorable that the N.S.P. used black and white patrol cars from that date until 1963 when they changed to all white.

A 1940 Ford sedan of the Florida Highway Patrol.

In April 1940 the Missouri State Highway Patrol Safety Squadron took to the highways. It was the only unit of its kind in the United States. Its two-fold purpose was traffic enforcement and public education. It consisted of 13 motorcycle officers and one officer to operate a mobile headquarters, a trailer, pulled by a 1940 Ford coupe.

A spotless Indian motorcycle of the New York City police, about 1940.

A 1941 Buick coupe of the California Highway Patrol. The officer on the left appears to be a motorcycle officer.

This sleek 1941 Oldsmobile coupe served with the California Highway Patrol.

A 1941 Ford sedan of the Pennsylvania Motor Police, later known as State Police.

A 1941 DeSoto of the Nebraska Safety Patrol photographed at an inspection at Camp Ashland. Camp Ashland was the original training site of the N.S.P.

Two separate aerials on this 1942 Chrysler Saratoga indicate the car was equipped with a two-way radio. This car was used by the California Highway Patrol when they were still a part of the Department of Motor Vehicles.

The car on the left is a 1942 Pontiac and the one on the right is a 1941 Ford. Both were used by the Florida Highway Patrol.

This woman, possibly a Red Cross volunteer, lifts the hood of a 1942 Ford belonging to the Texas Highway Patrol.

This 1942 Plymouth was photographed at the courthouse in Minneapolis, Minn.

A brand new 1942 Plymouth, photographed at the factory, prepares to begin service with the Michigan State Police.

The Oakland, Calif. police traffic squad pass in review in 1944.

U.S. Army military policemen pose with their jeep in Berlin, Germany in 1945. When World War II ended, allied military police were responsible for maintaining civil order in the decimated German cities.

The Omaha, Neb. Police Department had black and white patrol cars in the 1940s as shown by this 1946 Ford. The door emblem is a copy of the O.P.D. badge that was adopted in 1941. It is a sunburst topped by a buffalo.

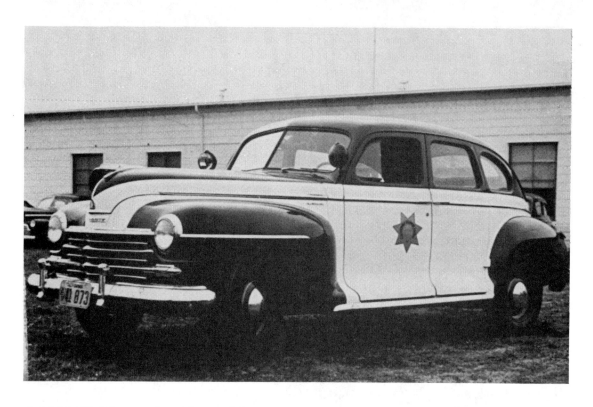

A 1946-'48 Plymouth of the California Highway Patrol. The one clear and one red spotlight has practically become a trademark of the C.H.P. This arrangement of spotlights is still used today by the agency.

This California Highway Patrol officer stands beside his 1946 Buick patrol car.

Although this 1946 Pontiac doesn't appear to have any markings, the spotlight and siren/red light combination leave little doubt as to what the car is.

This photo shows a 1946 Mercury four-door sedan belonging to the California Highway Patrol.

A sergeant with the Missouri State Highway Patrol stands beside his 1946 Ford which is marked simply, "State Patrol."

This 1947 Mercury convertible was used by the Ohio Highway Patrol. It is unusual because convertibles are seldom used as patrol cars.

This Ford sedan and Harley-Davidson motorcycle show the new all white paint jobs the Colorado State Patrol vehicles adopted about 1947.

A line of brand new 1947 Fords of the Los Angeles Police Department.

A 1947 Ford of the Nebraska Safety Patrol.

This 1947 Plymouth of the Indianapolis, Ind. police appears to have been involved in an accident. Note the damage to the rear fender.

This 1947 Chevrolet belonging to the Idaho State Police featured eye-catching markings that are still in use today.

The Alaska Highway Patrol used this large Chrysler in 1947. They needed chains in that snow country.

In 1947 the California Highway Patrol became a separate department from the Department of Motor Vehicles. This 1947 Ford shows the new door emblem, a seven-point star.

A 1948 DeSoto belonging to the California Highway Patrol. That paint job really makes the front end look long!

This Alabama patrolman sits patiently while a photographer captures his 1947 Ford on film.

A 1948 Pontiac patrol car with an unusual door marking. This Pontiac served with the Hastings, Neb. Police Department.

The body configuration on this 1948 Chevrolet dictated that the door emblems be placed on the rear doors instead of the front doors where they are usually found. The Pima County, Ariz. Sheriff's Department used this car.

An officer of the Nassau County, N.Y. police with his 1948 Ford patrol car. Notice the call number on the side. Before the universal 911 number came into use, departments often put their local call number on their vehicles.

A Hastings, Neb. police officer poses proudly with his Indian motorcycle in 1948. A 1947 Ford patrol car provides the backdrop for this photo.

This is a photograph of the first transport vehicle for the New York City police mounted unit in 1948. The truck could carry six horses and equipment.

The Missouri State Highway Patrol adopted a new door marking in 1948, as displayed by this Chevrolet. This style door marking is still used today.

A 1948 Chevrolet coupe of the Oakland, Calif. Police Department.

A 1949 Ford "black and white" of the San Francisco police.

The Baltimore County, Md. police used this 1949 Chevrolet.

The Nassau County, N.Y. police used this 1949 Indian motorcycle.

This 1949 Ford of the Washington State Patrol has a paint scheme similar to its Nebraska counterpart of that year.

This Nebraska Safety Patrolman poses with his 1949 Ford in front of the Nebraska capitol building in Lincoln.

Troopers of the Georgia State Patrol pose with their 1949 Pontiac. This patrol car sported an eye-catching paint scheme.

A 1942 Plymouth of the Missouri State Highway Patrol.

This photograph shows a Wichita, Kan. policeman behind the wheel of his 1946 Ford. The door emblem used at this time was a copy of the Wichita police breast badge.

FLORIDA HIGHWAY PATROL

This 1949 Ford convertible was used in parades by the Florida Highway Patrol. The car was painted and furnished by the Ford Motor Co.

Apparently an experimental-type marking adorns this 1946 Ford of the Ohio State Highway Patrol.

This 1948 Buick of the Colorado State Patrol sports newly installed radio equipment.

The door emblems on this 1941 Ford matched the badges of the Dallas, Texas police at the time.

A California Highway Patrol officer poses with his 1948 Buick cruiser.

A large speaker adorns the roof of this 1949 Ford which was in service with the Wichita, Kan. Police Department.

Running from the law was no fun when the '49 Oldsmobile appeared on the scene. 1949 marked the year of the powerful new 307 cubic inch rocket V-8. The "Rocket 88s" proved formidable in patrol cars like this California Highway Patrol unit, as well as in stock car racing.

5

1950s

These San Francisco, Calif. police cars, two 1951 and one 1950 Ford, display the different door emblems used by the S.F.P.D.

A Ford, 1950 vintage, of the Colorado State Patrol.

This 1950 Dodge had no markings other than red grille lights and a spotlight. It was used by the Hastings, Neb. Police Department. The car beside it was the fire chief's car.

This 1950 Ford pickup was used to pull a Snowcat for the Colorado State Patrol.

One of three Snow Cats purchased by the Colorado State Patrol in 1949. These vehicles were used for rescue and maintenance of some of the high altitude radio relay stations.

This Kaiser-Manhatten would fit into the category of "odd" police cars. The Ohio Highway Patrol used this one around 1951.

1950 and 1951 Buicks of the Alaska Highway Patrol, taken at Fairbanks, Alaska.

The New York City Police Department periodically photographed, in a group, one of each type of vehicle they used. This photo, taken on Randall Island in 1951, shows the variety of vehicles this large department had at the time. Today the variety has grown even larger. Shown in this photo are: a 1950 Plymouth two-door patrol car, a 1950 Plymouth unmarked detective car, a two-wheeled motorcycle, a three-wheeled motorcycle with sidecar, a mobile laboratory, a mounted unit horse van, a Chevrolet loudspeaker panel truck, a 1949 Ford emergency services car, an emergency services rescue truck, a bomb disposal tractor-trailer, a field headquarters truck, a stake truck, an International prisoner van, a harbor precinct launch service truck, a tow truck, a 1950 Chevrolet station wagon, C Chevrolet panel truck, and a Dodge communications division panel truck.

Nassau County, N.Y. police unit 502, a 1951 Pontiac, at an unknown call.

This 1951 Ford of the Lincoln, Neb. Police Department was black with a white stripe starting at the very front-center of the hood and running down both sides at the top of the doors.

A front view of Lincoln, Neb. police '51 Ford showing stripe.

This black and white 1951 Ford was used by the Washington State Patrol.

A 1952 Ford of the Los Angeles, Calif. police parked at city hall.

A Missouri state trooper poses with his 1952 Chevrolet.

This 1952 Ford of the Colorado State Patrol looks like it would be easy to lose in a snowdrift!

A mechanic prepares a "new" 1952 Ford for the Nebraska Safety Patrol. Note the light in the center part of the grille.

1953 Ford station wagon with the Milwaukee, Wis. police.

These 1953 Chevrolets of the Oakland, Calif. Police Department had different paint schemes.

A 1953 Chevrolet paddy wagon of the Detroit, Mich. Police Department.

A Dallas, Texas policeman loads a prisoner into a 1953 Chevrolet paddy wagon.

A Florida Highway Patrolman with his 1953 Pontiac cruiser.

A 1953 Chevrolet of the Wyoming Highway Patrol.

This all black 1953 Pontiac of the Nassau County, N.Y. police featured orange wheels.

A 1954 Chevrolet of the Milwaukee, Wis. Police Department.

This factory brochure for the 1953 Ford advertises the 125 hp "Interceptor" V-8 flat-head engine, which was available at extra cost.

1954 Ford sedan deliveries like this one of the Alaska Territorial Police often did double duty as patrol cars and ambulances.

This U.S. Army military police car is a 1954 Ford. The "HP" door emblem denoted that it was a highway patrol car. The U.S. military police provided these patrol functions in Germany for many years after World War II.

Belmont, Calif. police personnel pose with cycles and 1954 Plymouth patrol cars.

A North Carolina state trooper monitors traffic with a new "Electronic Speed Clock." His unit is a 1954 Ford.

Detroit, Mich. officials inspect "new" 1955 DeSoto patrol cars.

This Alaska Territorial policeman poses beside his 1954 Ford sedan in his shirt sleeves. It must be summer.

These San Francisco, Calif. police 1955 Fords are not marked with the traditional "SFPD" stars because they belong to the Bay Cities traffic Accident Investigation Bureau.

The Bakersfield, Calif. police used this Jeep around 1955.

Although the sign on the front fender of this motorcycle says "Police," this is a Colorado State Patrol unit around 1955.

This lineup of New Jersey State Police vehicles includes a 1954 Buick, a 1956 Ford, a 1955 Ford, a 1955 Ford wagon and an early 1950s Chevrolet truck.

A time honored 1955 Chevrolet in service with the Bakersfield, Calif. police.

This photo shows a 1955 Ford of the Missouri State Highway Patrol. The trooper exhibits the "proper tip" of the campaign hat.

Oakland, Calif. police used 1956 Fords like this one.

A 1956 Ford sedan delivery of the Washington State Patrol.

Missouri State Patrolmen pose with a new fleet of 1956 Dodge patrol cars.

Kansas City, Mo. police sergeants check over the equipment in their 1956 Ford. The door marking indicates that the car was used specifically by "field sergeants."

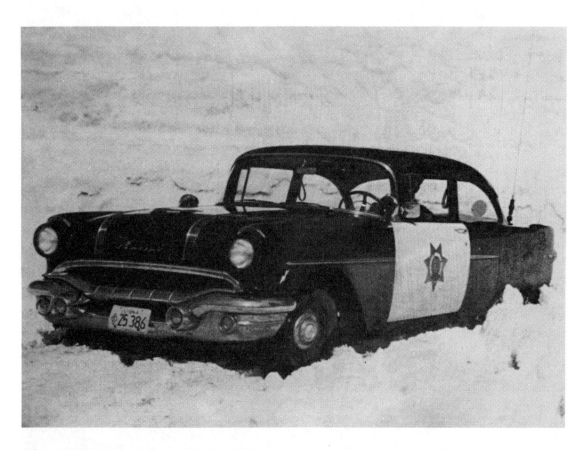

This 1956 Pontiac of the California Highway Patrol was photographed in a setting that more closely resembles Nebraska in the winter!

The photographer had a scenic background when he shot this 1956 Oldsmobile of the Arizona Highway Patrol.

Two Nebraska Safety Patrolmen pose with their 1956 Ford.

A 1956 Ford Ranch Wagon of the Kansas City, Mo. Police Department. This laboratory unit was used for crime scene work. "This new vehicle provides greater maneuverability, ventilation that protects sensitive equipment on hot days, and capacity for locked containers for the equipment."

This 1957 Ford belonged to the Colorado State Patrol.

This 1957 Cadillac police ambulance belonged to the Milwaukee Police Department.

A Bakersfield, Calif. police officer uses the radio in his 1957 Ford.

This Dallas, Texas policeman strikes a formidable pose with his 1957 Ford patrol car.

Hastings, Neb. police officers pose in 1957 with the department's two cars, a 1957 Plymouth and a 1956 Chevrolet.

A public relations display of the Kansas City, Mo. police features a 1957 Ford patrol car. Note rifle, sub-machine gun and shotgun on floor.

This 1957 Ford of the New York City Police Department was assigned to one of the "motorcycle" precincts, which are today "highway patrol" units. This car performed special duty in traffic safety awareness. The roof-mounted speedometer could be easily seen by motorists, reminding them of their speed, and that speed kills. These devices were used by many traffic law enforcement agencies around the country.

1958 and '59 Plymouths fill the lot at the San Mateo, Calif. Police Department. Do you think they could be discussing where to head for coffee and doughnuts?

A 1957 Plymouth police car brochure.

"Super powered up to 290 horsepower," states the information from this 1957 Plymouth brochure. This car was built for "action."

A classic today, this 1957 Chevrolet was used by the Washington State Patrol.

Wichita, Kan. police used this 1958 Ford cruiser.

A patrolman with the North Carolina State Highway Patrol poses with his 1958 Ford cruiser.

This lineup of Milwaukee, Wis. police units includes a paddy wagon, Cadillac ambulance and three 1958 Plymouths.

The Ocean County, N.J. Sheriff's Department used this 1958 Chevrolet station wagon. There would be no mistaking who this car belonged to with the bold "Sheriff" marking on the hood.

A Nebraska safety patrolman at the Lincoln headquarters with his 1958 Dodge.

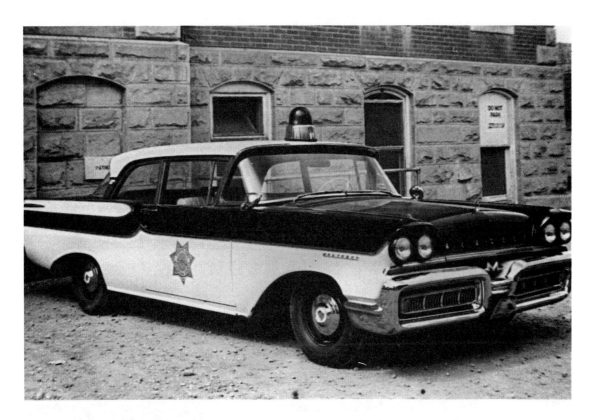

This sleek 1958 Mercury features a unique black and white paint scheme. This car was used by the Jefferson County, Colo. Sheriff's Department.

A 1959 Ford Ranch Wagon of the Milwaukee, Wis. police.

A factory brochure for the 1958 Ford police cars.

A 1958 Plymouth police car brochure.

According to the brochure, "Every police officer would be proud to drive the '58 Plymouth."

This photo, taken from the brochure, shows the 1958 Plymouth Savoy police car.

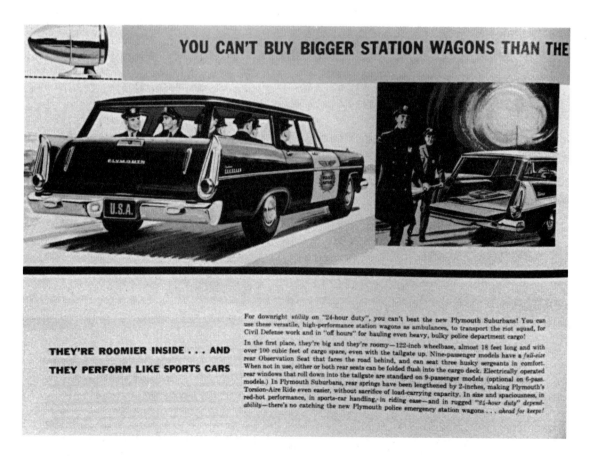

The 1958 Plymouth Suburban police emergency wagon from the brochure.

Alabama state troopers with their 1959 Chevrolets.

An Idaho state policeman with his flashy 1959 Ford patrol car.

The Missouri State Highway Patrol used both two- and four-door 1959 Dodges.

A 1959 Dodge of the California Highway Patrol, shown here with a Cessna 172 airplane that was leased by the agency.

This 1959 Dodge of the California Highway Patrol had an extended career after being retired from patrol duty. In this photo a cadet takes it through the skid pan at the C.H.P. academy.

By 1959 the Alaska Territorial Police had changed to Alaska State Police. Shown here is a 1959 Ford.

This photo is an International Metro van which served as a paddy wagon for the San Francisco, Calif. Police Department.

Three-wheeled motorcycles, like this Bakersfield, Calif. unit, were generally used for parking enforcement duties.

This Oldsmobile apparently shared the bid with a Pontiac in 1956 for the California Highway Patrol.

A 1959 Ford belonged to the Ohio Highway Patrol.

Dallas, Texas police used Fords through the middle 1950s such as this 1955 model.

Ex-military vehicles, such as this Dodge four-wheel drive pickup, were sometimes employed for special uses. This truck belonged to the Colorado State Patrol.

Two 1951 Fords used by the Illinois State Police.

This 1959 Ford of the Alabama Highway Patrol was adorned with state-shaped door emblems.

This photo shows the equipment carried in the Army Military Police highway patrol Ford.

6

1960s

A 1960 Dodge police car brochure.

DODGE DART AND '60 DODGE POLICE PURSUITS

118" WHEELBASE—LIGHT, COMPACT, NIMBLE!

DODGE DART 2-DOOR POLICE PURSUIT

DODGE DART 4-DOOR POLICE PURSUIT

122" WHEELBASE—BIG, BRAWNY, POWERFUL!

DODGE DART STATION WAGON POLICE PURSUIT

'60 DODGE 2-DOOR POLICE PURSUIT
(Available also in '60 DODGE 4-DOOR POLICE PURSUIT)

SPECIAL NOTE: '60 Dodge Police Pursuits are available on special order volume purchases only.
NOTE: Illustrations of 118" WB Dodge Dart Police Pursuits are of the Seneca series.
118" WB 2- and 4-door sedans are also available in the lower cost Seneca Fleet model.

The policy of Dodge Division of Chrysler Corporation is one of continued improvement in design and manufacture wherever possible to assure a still finer car. Hence, specifications, equipment and prices are subject to change without notice.

DODGE DIVISION • CHRYSLER CORPORATION

12-59—Police Brochure

Variations of the 1960 Dodge police cars from the brochure.

This brand new 1960 Plymouth went to work with the Ohio State Highway Patrol. The car was equipped with Plymouth's "Golden Commando" V-8, a 361 cubic inch engine with 305 horsepower.

A 1960 Chevrolet Biscayne two-door sedan of the Ohio State Highway Patrol.

The cover of this factory brochure on 1960 Fords features a Kansas City, Mo. police unit. An inline six-cylinder engine, specifically geared toward economy minded departments, was one choice available.

This selection of patrol cars was used by the Alaska State Police. From left to right: 1960 Ford, 1960 Ford, 1961 Chevrolet, 1959 Ford and 1957 Ford.

Officers of the New York State Police with their 1960 Plymouths and motorcycles.

A Colorado state patrolman poses alongside the highway with his 1960 Ford.

A Wichita, Kan. policeman gives assistance. His patrol car is a 1960 Ford.

This 1960 Chevrolet "black and white" features a black body with white doors, hood and trunk.

Nebraska safety patrolmen with their 1960 Dodges. A 1958 Chevrolet is in the center. All of their '58 Chevys had to have their brake systems refitted by General Motors because of recurring brake failures.

These all white 1960 Plymouths were used by the Arizona Highway Patrol.

A 1960 Dodge police pursuit of the California Highway Patrol. Powered by a 383 cubic inch Special Police Pursuit V-8, this engine was selected by California and Missouri Highway Patrols after competitive testing of engines over 400 cubic inch displacement. The engine was capable of a 325 horsepower output.

A long line of Wichita, Kan. policemen pose with their 1961 Dodge patrol cars.

This factory photo is of a 1961 Dodge police car. Dodge offered four specially designed 1961 police cars with a choice of six engines. Two- and four-door sedan models were specially equipped for highway, general or municipal patrol use. A public safety station wagon was also available. The six Dodge engines were: a 383 cubic inch, ram-induction V-8 recommended for highway patrol cars; a 383 cubic inch, 325 horsepower Special Police Pursuit V-8 recommended for highway patrol cars; a 361 cubic inch, 305 horsepower D-500 V-8 recommended for highway patrol cars and station wagons; a 318 cubic inch, 260 horsepower V-8 recommended for general purpose cars and station wagons; a 318 cubic inch, 230 horsepower V-8 recommended for general purpose and municipal patrol cars and station wagons; and a 225 cubic inch, 145 horsepower Slant Six recommended for municipal police use and station wagons. All Dodge police cars had unitized bodies and were given a seven-step dip and spray anti-corrosion treatment.

A 1961 Plymouth and trooper photographed at the Kentucky State Police Academy.

This 1962 Plymouth station wagon served the Detroit, Mich. Police Department.

This Nebraska Safety Patrolman poses with his 1962 Ford, the last of the N.S.P.'s black and white cars.

A Kern County, Calif. sheriff's sergeant prepares to start patrolling in his 1962 Plymouth.

This 1962 Chevrolet waits patiently for its next shift with the Wisconsin State Patrol.

Hastings, Neb. policemen pose with their units. From left to right: 1962 Chevrolet, 1961 Ford, 1961 Chevrolet.

Missouri State Patrolmen with a 1963 Ford cruiser. The winged emblem on the fender indicates engine size, possibly a 390 cubic inch model.

A 1963 Chevrolet of the Iowa Highway Patrol.

A 1963 Ford and airplane of the North Carolina Highway Patrol.

This Kansas Highway Patrolman poses with his 1963 Chevrolet.

A 1964 Dodge police car brochure.

Variations that were available of the standard '64 Dodge, from the brochure.

From the '64 Dodge police car brochure, the "Big Dodge 880."

This 1964 Ford served with the Pennsylvania State Police.

A 1964 Dodge 880 of the Missouri State Highway Patrol. A massive 413 cubic inch engine was available in this model that put out 360 horsepower.

The San Francisco City Hall furnishes the backdrop for this photo of a San Francisco Police Department 1965 Ford.

The interior of this San Francisco Police Department '65 Ford shows a switch panel for operating emergency lights, a Motorola two-way radio and a shotgun mount.

The Wichita, Kan. police used this 1965 Plymouth. Engine offerings of the '65 Plymouth police cars ranged from a 145 horsepower 225 cubic inch six-cylinder to a 330 horsepower 383 cubic inch V-8.

Chrysler Corp. factory brochure on the 1965 Dodge Polara Police Pursuit.

Chrysler Corp. factory brochure on the 1965 Plymouth Police Specials.

A Kansas City, Mo. police officer and his Harley-Davidson Electra Glide, circa 1965.

A Detroit, Mich. police officer and his new 1965 Plymouth pose with a replica Detroit Police Department 1920s Ford Model T. The Model T is a replica of the first known police radio car. Note the primitive antenna on the roof.

A U.S. Army military policeman takes time out for a photo with his 1965 Ford Fairlane.

A sharp 1966 Dodge of the Nevada Highway Patrol.

A Virginia State Police officer poses with his 1966 Ford.

A factory brochure on the 1966 Ford police package cars.

Chrysler Corp. factory brochure on the 1966 Dodge Police Pursuits.

A 1966 Ford of the Detroit, Mich. Police Department.

1966 also marked the first year of all white patrol cars for Dallas, Texas police. Shown are a black 1965 Ford and a white 1966 Chevrolet.

A 1966 Ford of the Washington State Patrol. Displayed beside it is the equipment it carried.

This New York City police car served with Motorcycle Precinct #1 in the Bronx. The 1967 Plymouth was outfitted with removable window screens and Plexiglas windshield insert for use in civil distrubances.

In 1967 the Nebraska Safety Patrol used these two-door Chevrolets which were equipped with a powerful 396 cubic inch engine. When these cars were retired, they were eagerly sought after by hot rodders.

The California Highway Patrol tried out some Oldsmobile patrol cars as shown by this 1967 model.

1968 Plymouth police car brochure.

A California Highway Patrol 1968 Dodge. The push bars on the front end enabled the patrolman to remove a motorist's broken-down car when it was too dangerous to wait for a tow truck.

From the brochure, a 1968 Plymouth Fury "Patroller."

Oldsmobiles have never been highly used as patrol cars. This 1968 model was used by the Illinois State Police.

This 1968 Chevrolet of the Suffolk County, N.Y. police was a K-9 unit. Metal screen over rear door windows gave the dog fresh air, but offered protection for over-enthusiastic onlookers.

This unusual police car, a 1969 Cadillac, saw service with the Howard County, Neb. Sheriff's Department as late as 1987.

A 1969 Dodge of the California Highway Patrol.

An accident scene in Hastings, Neb. Note the old style radar unit mounted on the side of this 1969 Plymouth police car.

The Newark, N.J. police traffic division used this 1969 Chevrolet.

7

1970-Present

The Wilmington, Del. police used Chevrolets and AMC Ambassadors such as this one in the early 1970s.

The Pontiac Lemans was offered with police options in the late 1970s. This one served in California.

A popular patrol car of the late '70s was the Chevrolet Nova.

The Suffolk County, N.Y. police used this 1970 Chevrolet station wagon, which awaits repair in the department's storage lot.

This Dodge Demon would fit into the category of "uncommon" patrol cars.

This prominently marked 1971 Chevrolet belonged to the Jersey City, N.J. police.

Pontiacs were used by the Hastings, Neb. Police Department in 1971.

A Washington State Patrolman poses with his 1971 Dodge.

A 1971 Dodge police brochure, "Here's the Ticket for Police Duty."

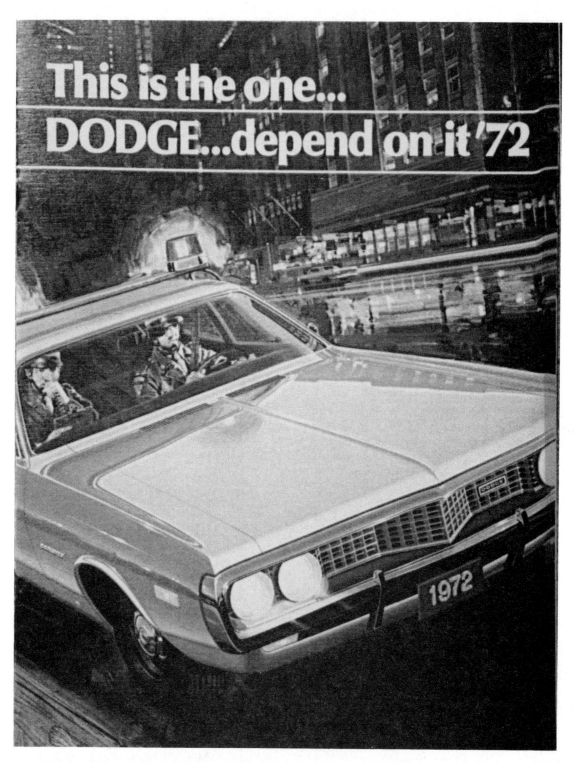

A Chrysler Corp. factory brochure for the '72 Dodge police cars.

This 1972 Plymouth of the Suffolk County, N.Y. police is equipped with a public address speaker mounted on the front fender.

This '73 Dodge Polara had an unusual green and white paint scheme. The car was used by the Bethel, Conn. police.

A 1974 Plymouth Fury I of the New Hampshire State Police.

The blue and yellow colors of this 1974 Plymouth Satellite were used by the Nassau County police from 1973 to 1977. In 1978 this department's cars were all white.

The Alabama State Troopers used this AMC Javelin in 1974.

This big Dodge Monaco is a 1975 model.

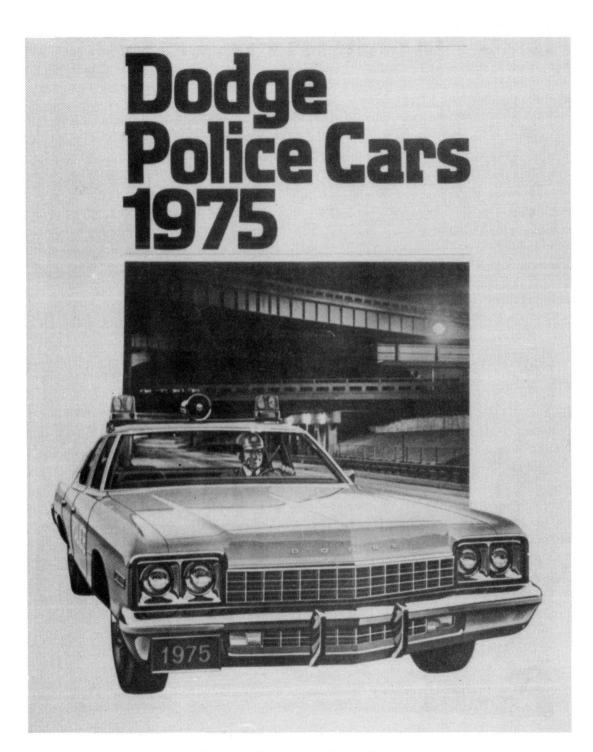

Chrysler Corp. factory brochure on the 1975 Dodge police cars.

1975 PLYMOUTH POLICE CARS

A Chrysler Corp. factory brochure for the 1975 Plymouth police cars.

This 1976 Chevrolet Impala was used by the Washington State Patrol.

The Nevada Highway Patrol used this '78 Plymouth Fury.

The Michigan State Police used Chevrolet Caprices. Note unusual sign mounted on hood.

Close-up of "Stop" sign on Michigan State Police Chevy. These unusual signs can be lighted for use at night.

A Pontiac Parisienne station wagon in service with the New Mexico State Police.

Police in New Albany, Ind. use this Chevrolet Chevette for traffic work.

This black and white cruiser is an Oldsmobile Cutlass. It was used by the Berea, Ohio police.

A Chevrolet Celebrity of the Salt Lake City, Utah Police Department.

One of several cars being tested for Ford by the Arizona Highway Patrol is this Probe.

The Springfield, Ohio police use this Chevrolet Cavalier.

Also tested by the California Highway Patrol were Ford Fairmonts.

This Ford of the Oklahoma Highway Patrol was apparently used by a troop commander.

The Washington, D.C. police used this Chevrolet station wagon.

A Chevrolet Celebrity of the Federal Protective Service in Washington, D.C. These officers guard federal complexes including the FBI building.

Foreign cars are nothing new to American law enforcement. This Saab was used by the Pitkin County, Colo. Sheriff's Department.

The Tallahassee, Fla. police used this Pontiac Phoenix.

Four-wheel drive vehicles are common in Central City, Colo. This AMC Eagle was used by the Gilpin County Sheriff's Department.

This Volvo was used by the police in Augusta, Maine.

A Chevrolet Caprice of the Montana Highway Patrol.

This Chevrolet was used by the Albany, Ga. Police Department.

An Alaska State Trooper poses with her Plymouth Gran Fury. Short sleeves in Alaska?

This Dodge Diplomat is equipped for use in heavy traffic areas. The equipment includes a sturdy push bumper on the front and a light bar that can be raised to warn motorists of trouble well in advance.

A Dodge Diplomat of Montana's capital city, Helena.

Ever wonder what the police cars look like in the most famous of all old west towns? Well, here it is, a Chevrolet patrol car of the Dodge City, Kan. Police Department.

This Vermont State Police Chevrolet is green with gold stripes.

The markings of this Indiana State Police Ford are quite striking.

This Ford LTD of the U.S. Park Police was photographed at the base of the Washington Monument in Washington, D.C.

The F-4 Phantom aircraft makes an interesting backdrop for this photo of a U.S. Air Force Security Police Ford. Photo was taken at open house activities at the headquarters of the Strategic Air Command in Omaha, Neb.

A Ford Crown Victoria of the Houston, Texas police.

A handsomely marked Ford LTD of the East Palo Alto, Calif. Police Department.

The U.S. Border Patrol started a program called, "Project Roadrunner." The program utilized a Ford Mustang, Pontiac Trans Am and Chevrolet Z-28 Camaro (pictured) as pursuit cars on highways in the southwestern part of the United States.

The Ford Taurus found its way into police work even before the official "police package" version was released. This standard Taurus was used by the Fillmore County, Neb. Sheriff's Department.

This Georgia trooper is no doubt proud of his "ride," a Pontiac Trans Am.

The employees of the Baltimore County, Md. police garage apparently think Corvettes would be good patrol cars! This car was decked out with emblems and red light for photo purposes.

A Dodge Mirada of the Belle Fourche, S.D. Police Department.

A personally owned patrol car of the Bernalillo County, N.M. Sheriff's Department. Spending a shift in this Monte Carlo SS wouldn't be too bad!

An unusual patrol car, this Checker was used by the Woodlake, Calif. police.

This Missouri State Trooper poses along the road with his Mercury Marquis.

A Plymouth Reliant (K-car) in use by the New York City Franchise Bureau.

This Chevrolet Caprice of the Minnesota State Patrol is a striking red in color. Their cruiser colors are traditionally maroon, which corresponds with the trooper's uniforms.

The San Diego Naval Station police use this Ford LTD as a K-9 unit.

Although not yet available in a police package, the Ogalalla, Neb. police bought a Dodge Dynasty. Even though used mainly by administrative personnel, the department is happy with it.

The Chevrolet Caprice for 1991 is completely redesigned. This unit was recently acquired by the Bellevue, Neb. Police Department. It had yet to have light bar fitted when this photo was taken.

The Bloomfield, N.J. police use this sleek Toyota Celica Supra.

This officer works for the police department in world famous Boys Town, Neb. He was photographed in 1985 with his Ford Crown Victoria cruiser.

The police in Oyster Bay Cove, N.Y. seem to like Oldsmobiles. This one is an '85 Cutlass.

An '86 Ford Tempo of the Dunsmuir, Calif. police.

This shiny Mustang belongs to the Florida Highway Patrol.

Motorists of West Virginia should beware of troopers bearing Dodge Daytonas! Heads are turned regularly with this beauty.

An inside shot of the West Virginia State Police's '87 Dodge Daytona.

A Mustang of the Wisconsin State Patrol.

This Eureka, Calif. police Mustang is evidence that highway patrol agencies aren't the only ones using this popular car.

Mustangs are also popular in the Hawaiian Islands, as shown by this Maui County police unit.

This Mustang of the Nevada Highway Patrol is fitted with a unique light bar.

A Mustang of the Nebraska State Patrol.

This Texas Highway Patrol Mustang uses front mounted grille lights instead of roof-mounted light bar.

This Mustang is being used by the Lancaster County, Neb. Sheriff's Department.

A Missouri State Highway Patrol Mustang.

If there is such a thing as an "elegant" cruiser, this Lincoln Continental Town Car of the Dearborn, Mich. Police Department is it!

8

Special Units

This GMC Jimmy of the Metropolitan Boston Transit Authority is a K-9 unit which is rigged to ride the rails.

An International Scout of the New York City Police Department Traffic Unit. This photo was taken in 1973 which is the year the department changed to light blue and white vehicles.

This Isuzu Trooper wears the door emblems of the Maui County, Hawaii Police Department.

Some of the most famous lawmen of the Old West, the United States Marshals, use modern mounts like this Chevrolet Blazer. This one is used in the District of Wyoming for escorting nuclear weapons convoys, which is one of the duties of modern marshals.

This is not what you might imagine when thinking of a highway patrol vehicle. This 4 X 4 Dodge pickup is for off-road use in California.

A four-wheel drive Ford pickup of the Oseola County, Fla. Sheriff's Department.

A Ford pickup in service with the Denver, Colo. Sheriff's Department.

Hearts be still! Yes, this is a Ferrari sporting a light bar and police markings. The car was reportedly a "donation" from local drug dealers in San Mateo, Calif.

A "German" Volkswagen van in the service with the U.S. Army Military Police.

This Chevrolet truck of the Nassau County, N.Y. police is equipped with large flood-lights for use at emergency scenes.

A Chevrolet crew cab truck used by the New York City Police Emergency Services Unit.

This Dodge truck of the New York City police is used mainly by the communications divisions. The "MT" designates "Motor Transport."

This truck, part of the New York City Police Mounted Unit, is a horse transport.

A traffic safety unit of the Montana Highway Patrol. Note light bar on semi-tractor's roof.

Truck One, of the New York City Police Emergency Services Unit. This truck had a Hollywood "counterpart" which was seen on the weekly TV series, "True Blue."

A Ford Bronco in service with the Lead, S.D. police.

This Ford Ranger pickup is in use by Lincoln, Neb. police as a K-9 unit.

Each Nebraska State Patrol troop area was issued a Chevrolet Blazer for use by the lieutenants. The three K-9 units of the Nebraska State Patrol also use Blazers.

This Army Personnel Carrier is now used by the Lenexa, Kan. police for emergency situations.

The Jeffersonville, Ind. police use this converted military ambulance for emergency situations.

A 1968 Cadillac ambulance of the Nassau County, N.Y. Police Department.

This ex-military armored vehicle is shown in use by the Kansas City, Mo. police. It is now used by the Missouri State Highway Patrol.

The Sheriff's Department of Douglas County, Neb. uses this fully tracked vehicle for rescue work.

A U.S. Air Force security police armored vehicle. An M60 machine gun is mounted on the top.

This photo, taken in 1973, is the New York Police Department bomb unit known as "Big Bertha." The bomb carrying portion is made of heavy steel woven mesh. It was created at the direction of Mayor Fiorello Laguardia following the deaths of two bomb squad detectives at the 1939-'40 New York World's Fair. The tractor and trailer have been replaced from time to time over the years, and the markings have changed since 1973. The cargo portion, however, continues to be used as the design has proven itself reliable.

A Chevrolet S-10 Blazer of the Nuckolls County, Neb. Sheriff's Department.

The smaller Chevrolet Blazer, the S-10 model, is popular in law enforcement, especially sheriff's departments. This S-10 is used by the Boulder County, Colo. Sheriff's Department.

The Culver City, Calif. police apparently have a variety of vehicles, including Nissan pickups and this El Camino.

This El Camino appears to have seen some hard use with the Salt Lake City, Utah police.

This New York City police step van is used for transporting prisoners.

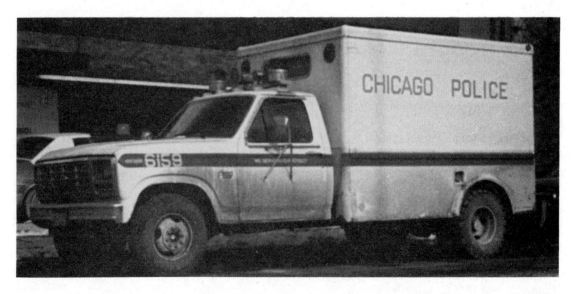

A Ford paddy wagon of the Chicago, Ill. police.

This large Dodge Power Wagon is used by the Fremont, Calif. police as a field headquarters.

This 1957 Ford armored truck saw service with the Washington, D.C. police.

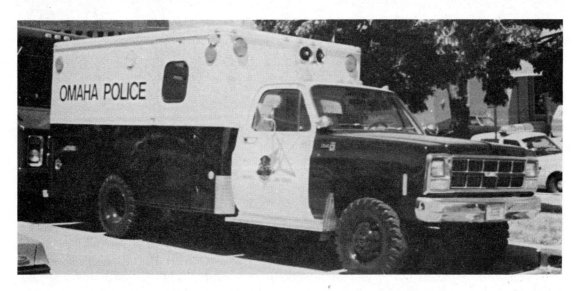

This four-wheel drive GMC truck is used by the police in Omaha, Neb.

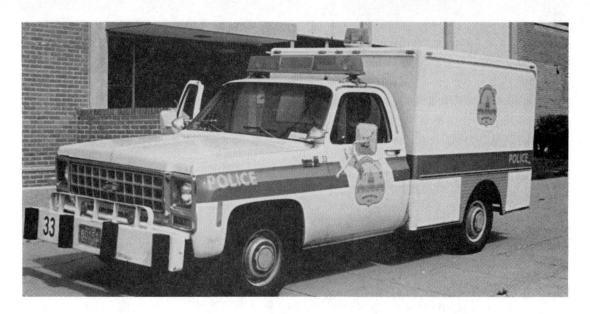

The police in our nation's capital use this Chevrolet truck for prisoner transport.

A Chevy truck used by the U.S. Park Police in Washington, D.C. for prisoner transport.

This modular Chevy van is used for explosive investigation by the Bureau of Alcohol, Tobacco, and Firearms Division of the Department of the Treasury. When needed, this truck is transported by a U.S. Coast Guard aircraft to U.S. possessions for investigations.

The United States Marshal for the Southern District of New York used this International bus for prisoner transport in 1974.

The Tallahassee, Fla. police used this large bus as a mobile command unit.

The Baltimore, Md. police use this motor home in crime prevention work.

This Diamond T bus resembles the "War Wagon." Note hydraulic gun turret and gun ports. This unit was used by the Illinois State Police.

This Plymouth Trail Duster was used by the New York City police in the 1970s.

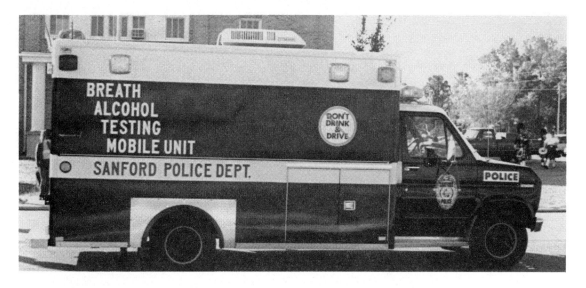

A new type of special unit is in use by many departments around the country. They're commonly nicknamed "Bat-Mobile" or "Bat Van" for "Breath Alcohol Testing" unit. The use of these vehicles allows officers to administer breath tests in the field. This B.A.T. unit is used by the Sanford, Fla. police.

The Special Operations Unit of the Boston, Mass. police use this Chevrolet stake truck for transporting barricades to needed areas.

The Honolulu, Hawaii Police use this Dodge Ramcharger.

A Chevrolet Suburban of the Nassau County, N.Y. Police Mounted Unit.

This Jeep Wagoneer served as a mounted unit transport for the Philadelphia, Pa. police.

A 1960s Jeepster used as a beach patrol unit by the Suffolk County, N.Y. Police Department.

The door marking on this Jeep Wagoneer leaves little doubt as to what it is. The vehicle belongs to the Greenbelt, Md. police.

This Jeep patrols the beautiful beaches of Miami Beach, Fla.

The Jeep Cherokees in two-and-four-door versions have become popular in police work. This one is a commerical vehicle enforcement unit of the Irvine, Calif. Police Department.

The Chenango County, N.Y. Sheriff's Department uses this Dodge Ramcharger.

This early 1970s Ford Econoline van has seen its better days. It was used by the Medford, Mass. police.

This ex-postal Jeep sports a police cap for his duties with the Boston police "Officer Friendly" program.

Postal Jeeps like this one are used by the Tallahassee, Fla. police.

This 1975 Dodge Ramcharger served as the first police K-9 unit in Lincoln, Neb.

The New York City police utilize many Cushmans like these for traffic work.

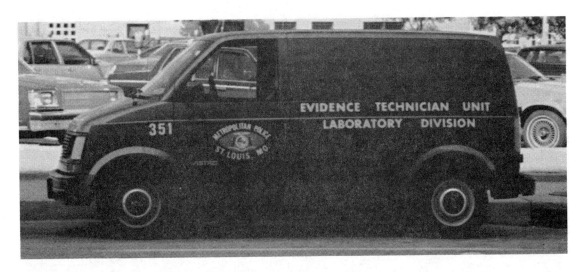

The St. Louis, Mo. police use this Chevy Astro van as an Evidence Technician Unit.

This Dodge Maxi-van is used by the United State Marshals Service for transportation of prisoners.

The window screens on this Ford van make its use obvious. The New York City Correction Department uses these for prisoner transport.

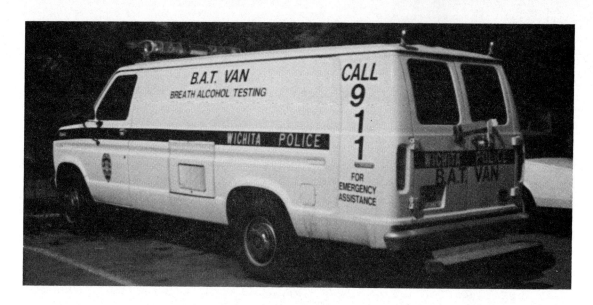

A Breath Alcohol Testing (B.A.T) van of the Wichita, Kan. Police Department.

A Volkswagen Beetle of the Scituate, Mass. police.

A Volkswagen Beetle outfitted for public relations work for the Somerville, Mass. police.

This New York City sanitation officer uses a Lambretta scooter.

One of the most famous "personalities" of the motorcycle field, the Harley-Davidson Electra Glide. This one was used by Suffolk County, N.Y. police.

A Chevrolet wrecker used by the Boston Police Fleet Services Division.

A Dodge Caravan K-9 unit of the U.S. Secret Service Uniformed Division at the White House in Washington, D.C.

The Massachusetts Capital Police find this Chevrolet Astro van a handy transporter of personnel.

This formidable appearing armored truck is used by the Virginia State Police.

U.S. Air Force Security Police Jeep, this one is a K-9 unit.

This International is classified as a "small" bomb disposal unit in the Nassau County, N.Y. Police Department.

This Ford Bronco, of the Idaho State Police, is equipped with rescue equipment including a front-mounted winch.

This Dodge Caravan is used by the New York-New Jersey Port Authority Police.

This sharp Chevrolet Astro van is used by the D.A.R.E. officers of the Lincoln, Neb. Police Department. The van was donated by a local cable television company. D.A.R.E. (Drug Abuse Resistance Education) is a nationwide program where school children are taught certain life skills such as esteem building and ways to avoid drugs.

A GMC Sierra of the Maryland, Mass Transit Administration Police.

After a military career, this four-wheel drive Dodge truck saw service with the San Luis Obispo County, Calif. Sheriff's Department.

A Communications Unit of the New York City Housing Police.

This Yamaha scooter is used by the New York City Police Department.

These 1986 Yamaha Sun Classics — gasoline-operated, two-cycle, 10 hp vehicles — were assigned to Denver, Colo.'s Stapleton International Airport. Denver police officers are assigned to the airport, and the vehicles were added to the airport fleet as patrol vehicles for the four-story parking structure. When the vehicles were new, they were used on a regular basis, but as they aged, the interest fell. At present, both are still assigned to the airport, however they are used very little.

This Electra Glide is shown in service of the Tucson, Ariz. police about 1970.

9

Restored Police Vehicles

Many people enjoy a bit of nostalgia in their lives, whether it's in music, clothing or automobiles. The photographs presented in this chapter will illustrate not only the nostalgic interest in vehicles, but the expanding hobby of restoring and owning a police vehicle.

Although this is not a new hobby, interest has increased greatly over the past 10 years. One explanation for this increase is that over the last decade, several state highway patrol agencies have celebrated their 50th anniversaries.

The vehicles have proven themselves as valuable assets to the department's public relations activities. Highway patrol agencies in California, Washington, Wisconsin, New Mexico, Mississippi, Minnesota, Florida, Oklahoma, Idaho, Missouri and Georgia, to name a few, maintain antique patrol vehicles. Crowds always seem to gather when they're displayed publicly.

Local law enforcement agencies have also put restored cruisers to work as effective public relations tools. They are not only valuable for public relations, but police officers learn to respect their own department's history and progress through the years.

These agencies aren't the only ones enjoying old official cars, however. More and more individuals own restored cruisers and surprisingly, not all are cops! The Police Car Owners of America was formed in 1990 to organize police car enthusiasts nationwide.

Would-be enthusiasts should have no trouble in finding a "project car" as these old sedans are routinely passed over by collectors and hot-rodders. It's up to the hobbyist if the car chosen is actually a retired police car or if it's a standard sedan outfitted as a replica. Antiques are, of course, prized by their owners, but it's obvious there is a high interest in cars from 1960 or newer, too.

A small handful of car dealers across the country specialize in used police cars. The cars offered are usually no more than four years old. One of these dealers is Diversifleet Inc., of Kansas City, Kan. The company obtains vehicles from all over the United States, but many come from southern states where winters are mild and salt isn't used on the roads.

Although law enforcement agencies make up most of the company's customers, individuals can also purchase the highway cruiser of their dreams! The cars are completely reconditioned including any needed body work. These cars are great for the hobbyist whose cruiser also has to function as the family's grocery getter!

One word of caution when outfitting any car to appear as a law enforcement vehicle: Be sure to thoroughly check state and local laws governing these activities. For example, California state law says the car must be 1979 or older, door emblems and red lights must be covered or removed when on public streets, and the switch for the siren must be located under the hood. Don't neglect this important part of the hobby, which could cost you "time" and money.

The following photographs represent only a sample of the restored police vehicles existing today.

277

This restored 1948 Hudson police car was photographed in a small Iowa town in 1989. Photographer was apparently caught in the act, as he is shown "assuming the position"!

This 1936 Dodge is quite possibly the oldest police car in official use today. The Shasta County, Calif. Marshal's Department requires the deputies to use their own vehicles in the performance of their duties. One deputy, who is also a car buff, spent over a year and $10,000 to restore this car for duty use. Certain state standards had to be met, which required modern headlights, red lights, turn signals, a siren and seat belts to be installed in the old sedan.

Missouri State Highway Patrol markings adorn this restored 1976 Plymouth Gran Fury.

This 1931 Lincoln phaeton is owned by the San Francisco, Calif. Police Department. In 1931 the S.F.P.D. purchased seven new police cars, six Model A Fords at $435 each and the Lincoln phaeton for the chief. The Lincoln, priced at $4,400, cost more than 10 Model As. Presidents, generals, royalty, clergy, governors, mayors and other dignitaries visiting San Francisco have all been given an honor afforded to very few people, a ride in the police department's '31 Lincoln. The car's 384 cubic inch V-8 can develop 120 horsepower and this allows it to cruise with the best of today's cars. Even though the car cost a huge amount in 1931, the city seems to have gotten their money's worth as it has been in service for 60 years.

A 1936 Ford sedan of the Boise, Idaho Police Department. It was purchased in 1985 for $3,500 and restored by the Boise Police Association using specifications and parts provided by the Ford Motor Co. All parts, with the exception of two door handles, are original Ford parts. The paint (color and texture) was mixed according to original Ford colors for the 1936 model year. The mohair upholstery was manufactured to original Ford specs. The total cost of restoration was $10,000.

This 1960 Plymouth belongs to the Suffolk County, N.Y. Police Department. It was one of the original fleet of patrol cars when the department was organized in 1960.

The Idaho State Police maintain this 1976 Plymouth which was the last of their light blue and white colored cars.

A beautifully restored 1949 Ford of the North Carolina Highway Patrol.

This restored 1930 Ford Model A coupe is owned by a California Highway Patrol traffic officer. It represents a C.H.P. car of the early 1930s and is a crowd-pleaser when displayed at various public relations events.

Officers of District #3, Idaho State Police, rebuilt this 1947 Chevrolet patrol car.

In observance of its 50th anniversary, the Wisconsin State Patrol had this 1939 Ford patrol car restored.

This 1934 Harley-Davidson was restored by the trooper shown, who is outfitted in a uniform of the time. The motorcycle was used in the 50th anniversary celebration of the North Carolina Highway Patrol.

This 1935 Ford roadster was donated to a North Carolina state museum. 1935 was the first year North Carolina state patrolmen had the opportunity to use automobiles as well as motorcycles.

This immaculate 1967 Plymouth Belvedere was found in some weeds. It was nothing more than an empty shell. It had been a Kansas Highway Patrol car and was restored to its original condition. These 1967 Plymouth K.H.P. cars featured factory bucket seats.

Believe it or not, this 1980 Dodge is the daily transportation of its owners. When not on display at a show, the magnetic markings and red lights come off.

An attractively restored 1940 Ford sedan of the Florida Highway Patrol.

A 1940 Ford sedan delivery of the Washington State Patrol.

This handsomely restored 1938 Buick in California Highway Patrol trim gathers a crowd wherever it is displayed.

The fine GMC paddy wagon of the 1930s is evidently a project of a local Milwaukee, Wis. American Legion Post.

The Associated Highway Patrol of Arizona presented this restored 1931 Ford Model A sedan to the Arizona Highway Patrol. It is similar to the cars used in 1931 when the highway patrol was started. It is painted copper with black fenders, the copper signifying the state's production of copper.

This 1948 Chevrolet was restored as a Lawton, Okla. unit.

The Montana Highway Patrol bought this 1935 Ford coupe in Nebraska and restored it.

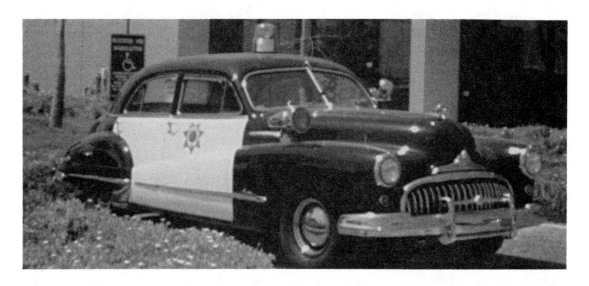

A restored 1948 Buick in the ever popular markings of the California Highway Patrol.

This splendid 1938 Nash Lafayette was restored to represent a car of the Palo Alto, Calif. Police Department.

Leon County, Fla. Sheriff's Department markings adorn this green and white 1953 Chevrolet. Green and white are colors still commonly found on Florida sheriff's vehicles.

This 1956 Chevrolet, photographed in 1974, appeared to still be in service with the Crazy Horse, S.D. police.

This 1946 Ford of the Delaware State Police participates in a parade.

One of the true classics of our time is the 1957 Chevrolet, restored in the official yellow of the Toronto, Canada police.

This restored 1954 Ford is painted brick red and white.

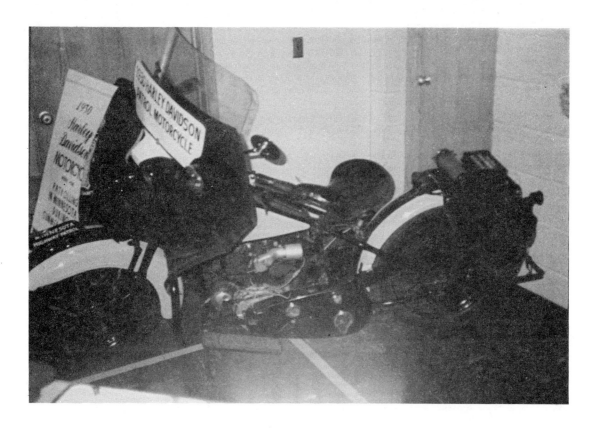

A restored 1930 Harley-Davidson motorcycle of the Minnesota Highway Patrol.

An early Ford Model T "C" cab paddy wagon.

A Ford Model A touring car is adorned with what could possibly be Chicago police markings of the day.

This restored 1935 Ford belongs to the Colorado State Patrol, which was originally named Courtesy Patrol.

This cleanly restored 1953 Chevrolet was located at a car dealer in York, Neb. The dealer purchased this restored car from an Indianapolis policeman. The officer had obtained the car at a city auction, then carefully searched out all the original equipment such as two-way radio, red lights, siren and door markings. These were all used to reinstate this car, which patrolled the streets of Indianapolis almost 40 years ago.

The door emblem on the restored 1953 Chevrolet.

The Alabama Department of Public Safety displays this 1936 Ford Highway Patrol car.

1978 Mercury at the Missouri Highway Patrol museum.

This beautifully restored 1957 Ford is displayed at various law enforcement functions by the owner.

Diversifleet Inc., of Kansas City, Kan., leased the Ford police car shown here which was one of several emergency vehicles leased to a movie production company. They appeared in the film, "Article 99."

1953 Chevrolet at the Missouri Highway Patrol museum.

A restored 1940 Chevrolet of the New Mexico State Police.

1959 Dodge at the Missouri Highway Patrol museum.

This Indiana State Police unit is a 1938 Chevrolet.

No, this immaculate 1960 Ford cruiser is not Sheriff Andy's patrol car from the popular television series. It was, however, leased by the owners for publicity photos when the movie "Return to Mayberry" began filming. This old Ford was in service with the Tustin, Calif. Police Department from 1960 to 1962. The red roof light was available as a special option direct from Ford.

This close-up of the interior of the 1960 Ford shows the old Motorola two-way radio and switch panel for the red lights and siren.

The 1960 Ford retains the original 223 cubic inch engine, termed the "Mileage Maker Six" in the 1960 police car brochure. The engine was rated at 145 horsepower.

The Iowa Highway Patrol (now State Patrol) was originated in 1935. This 1935 Ford and 1935 Indian motorcycle were restored in celebration of the department's 50th anniversary. The Iowa Highway Patrol started with 50 troopers who were each issued a cycle and patrol car. These vehicles had no radio so the troopers were instructed to phone in every hour!

This restored Indian motorcycle was one of the original Iowa Highway Patrol cycles.

The Los Altos, Calif. Police Officers Association restored this 1953 Ford.

The interior of the Los Altos '53 Ford shows a Motorola two-way radio of the time.

This restored New York City police speaker truck is a 1950 Ford.

The 1931 Ford Model A roadster at the Missouri Highway Patrol museum has a detachable face and trooper's hat it can wear when it becomes "Otto, the Talking Car." Youngsters can ask Otto questions dealing with safety and traffic laws.

This restored California Highway Patrol car is not only eye-catching, it fits into the category of "rare" automobiles. It is a 1955 Buick Century two-door sedan, one of only 268 made exclusively for the C.H.P. This unique Buick has the body of a Special two-door sedan, but from the firewall forward it is a Century model. It is powered by a 322 cubic inch V-8 engine capable of 236 horsepower.

The interior of this 1955 Buick is also faithfully restored, including a General Electric two-way radio of the period.

This restored patrol wagon was used by the New York City police. It is on display at their headquarters, One Police Plaza.

A 1950 Ford of the Nassau County, N.Y. Police Department.

This 1930s Harley-Davidson is on display at the California Highway Patrol Academy museum.

1942 Chevrolet at the Missouri Highway Patrol museum.

American Police Vehicles and Equipment — 1883-1991

1883 — Omaha, Neb. police purchase their first horse drawn patrol wagon.

1894 — Houston, Texas police spend $450 for their first horsedrawn patrol wagon.

1897 — Detroit, Mich. police institute a bicycle patrol, whose responsibility it is to apprehend speeding bicyclists.

1900 — Bicycle squad formed by Omaha, Neb. police.

1908 — First power-driven vehicle purchased by the Omaha, Neb. police, a White Steamer Auto Patrol Wagon.

1909 — San Francisco, Calif. police buy their first two patrol cars.

— Houston, Texas police place their first motorcycles (Harley-Davidsons) into service.

— Omaha, Neb. police purchases first police motorcycles.

1910 — Houston, Texas police purchase first patrol car.

1915 — San Francisco, Calif. police buys Ford Model Ts, some of which were converted to makeshift patrol wagons by building wooden cells on the rear. These were later equipped with hand-cranked sirens.

1921 — First Indian motorcycles used by the Washington State Patrol. They later used Harley-Davidsons with side cars.

— Idaho State Police officers are paid mileage for using personally owned motorcycles for patrol work.

— Detroit, Mich. police equip a Ford Model T touring car with a radio receiver, making the first radio patrol car.

1923 — Omaha, Neb. police use "pill boxes," police motorcycle-equipped outposts, which were located strategically around the city.

1927 — Washington State Patrol purchases its first patrol "wagon," a Ford panel delivery. W.S.P. officers use their own cars for patrol work.

— Houston, Texas police install their first commerical radio receivers in patrol cars. KPRC would interrupt regular programming to give out police calls.

1928 — Detroit, Mich. institutes first police broadcasting system, which used the call letters KOP."

1930 — San Francisco, Calif. police use Buick touring cars. Special squads of side car-equipped motorcycles called "Flying Squads" started. These were used for quick response to emergency calls.

1931 — Missouri State Highway Patrol purchases 36 Ford Model A roadsters for $413 each.

— Motorcycles are still primary vehicles for the Houston, Texas police.

1932 — Ford realizes the appeal its new V-8 engine has to law enforcement, so they marketed an open phaeton (four-door convertible) known as the "Police Special."

— California Highway Patrol purchases Ford five-window coupes equipped with the new powerful flathead V-8 engines.

— Honolulu, Hawaii Police Department initiates program where policemen own their own patrol cars for duty use. This system is still used today, but the H.P.D. does have department-owned marked units. The department owned units account for only 10 percent of the cars used, however.

1933 — Washington State Patrol begins using radios on their motorcycles. This era also shows the W.S.P. start to phase out motorcycles in favor of panel delivery type trucks.

— Missouri State Highway Patrol installs public broadcasting receivers that send out messages to patrolmen nine hours per day. Front-mounted red lights and door emblems appeared on W.S.P. vehicles about this time.

1934 — Idaho State Police purchases new Ford five-window coupes.

1935 — Colorado Courtesy Patrol (now "State Patrol") originated, at which time 17 motorcycles and 19 patrol cars were put into service.

1936 — Houston, Texas police install radio receivers in patrol cars.

— Idaho State Police purchase Dodge coupes.

— First "fixed" California Highway Patrol radio station established, using the call letters KAPI.

1937 — Georgia State Patrol buys its first patrol cars, 1937 Ford sedans for $710 each. These cars were gun-metal in color, with orange letters and bullet-proof windshields.

— First two-way radios installed in Houston, Texas police cars.

— Kansas Highway Patrol begins operation with 31 new Plymouth four-door sedans which were painted black with silver tops.

1940 — Nebraska Safety Patrol (later "State Patrol") undertakes a pilot project to make their black patrol cars more visable. The roof and hood of one car (a 1940 Chevrolet) is painted white and nicknamed "guinea pig." Public reaction if so favorable that all N.S.P. cars were painted black and white from then until 1963.

1941 — Ohio State Highway Patrol installs their first two-way radios in patrol cars.

1942 — Missouri State Highway Patrol installs two-way radios in their cars.

— Colorado State Patrol changes patrol car colors from the original silver and black to black and white.

1943 — Washington State Patrol installs two-way radios in all units.

1945 — Kansas Highway Patrol installs two-way radios in patrol cars.

1947 — California Highway Patrol becomes a separate agency. The round Department of Motor Vehicles door emblem is changed to the seven-point star emblem. (The words "Highway Patrol" weren't added above the star until 1960.)

1948 — Colorado State Patrol changes patrol car colors from black and white to all white.

— Federal Signal Corp. markets the "Beacon Ray," the first revolving emergency light.

1949 — Washington State Patrol replaces panel delivery-type vehicles with four-door sedans. Some panel deliveries were still used into the 1950s, however.

— California Highway Patrol place Oldsmobiles into service. These are equipped with powerful 307 cubic inch "Rocket 88" V-8 engines.

1951 — Chrysler Corp. introduces its high performance Hemi engine in Chryslers, Dodges and DeSotos.

1954 — Missouri State Highway Patrol places the first unmarked patrol cars used by the department into service. The 30 light blue cars were Fords, Dodges and Chevrolets.

— In 1953 Ford offered its flathead V-8 engine as a "Police Interceptor," however, the new interceptor in 1954, an overhead valve V-8, was more popular.

1955 — Federal Signal Corp. develops the first compact dash-mounted emergency light called the "Fireball".

— Plymouth, Chevrolet and Pontiac came out with new overhead valve V-8 engines, creating more competition for Ford in police car sales.

1956 — Ford introduces its new V-8 engine. The 312 cubic inch Interceptor engine is rated at 215 horsepower.

1957 — Plymouth's new V-8 engine is offered. The 318 cubic inch V-8 is rated at 290 horsepower and features an eight-barrel carburetion system. The 318 is offered in Chrysler-made cars through 1989.

1958 — Ford offers new 303 horsepower Police Interceptor V-8 engine. Precision fuel induction is featured on this 361 cubic inch engine.

1959 — Ford's top-of-the-line Police Interceptor engine is the 352 cubic inch V-8, rated at 300 horse-power.

1960 — Dodge's Special Police Pursuit V-8, a 325 horsepower 383 cubic inch V-8 engine, is popular with many agencies including the California Highway Patrol and the Missouri State Highway Patrol.

1962 — Dodge releases a totally redesigned and somewhat downsized sedan. The largest engine available in the new Dodge police car is the 361 cubic inch V-8, rated at 305 horsepower.

1964 — Federal Signal Corp. offers the first bar-mounted synchronized emergency lighting system called the "Visabar."

1967 — The California Highway Patrol purchases Oldsmobiles for patrol.

1969 — The Dodge Monaco equipped with the 440 Magnum engine is generally recognized as one of the fastest police cars ever. Some say it could reach speeds of 145-150 mph.

1972 — Nebraska State Patrol changes color of patrol cars from white to various colors.

1973 — New York City police change the colors of their long familiar black, white and green units to light blue and white.

1977-80 — New York City police experiment with compact cars that offered better gas mileage. Among the cars tried in patrol service were Plymouth Horizon, Chevrolet Citation and Ford Fairmont.

— California Highway Patrol experiments with smaller cars including Ford Fairmonts, Chevrolet Malibus, Plymouth Volare station wagons and Chevrolet Z-28 Camaros.

— The 1980 Dodge St. Regis obtains the dubious honor of being called one of the slowest police cars in modern history.

1982 — California Highway Patrol purchases 400 Ford Mustangs, at $6,868 each, for patrol duty.

1984 — Chrysler Corp. places a prototype Plymouth Reliant in service with the Washtenaw County, Mich. Sheriff's Department. The car features a turbo-charged 2.2 liter four-cylinder engine.

1986 — Chrysler Corp. attempts to market a turbo-charged, front-wheel drive Dodge 600 for law enforcement use, but it is not widely accepted.

1987 — California Highway Patrol begins a special low-visibility patrol program that zeroes in on commercial vehicle violations. A variety of cars are used, including front-wheel drive Chevrolet Celebrities. These units were painted various colors, but all retained the traditional white front doors with CHP markings.

1989 — Chevrolet drops the Celebrity police package.

— Non-traditional police cars are put into service by the Connecticut State Police. Unmarked cars including Ford Mustangs, Buick Regals and Grand Nationals, Mazda MX-6s and one Corvette are used.

— California Highway Patrol places a Toyota Camry into service for testing purposes.

— "Project Roadrunner" is initiated by the U.S. Border Patrol. Cars used for this project include Ford Mustang, Pontiac Trans Am and Camaro IROC Z-28.

1990 — Mid-size, front wheel drive Ford Taurus is offered with police package. The Taurus is powered by a 3.8 liter, fuel-injected V-6 engine.

1991 — Chevrolet introduces the Camaro RS with "Special Pursuit Package" to compete with the successful Ford Mustang.

— Nebraska State Patrol puchases small group of the Camaro police package cars.